Well Versed

Literary Works 2010

Foreword by Richard W. Jennings

Columbia Chapter
Missouri Writers' Guild

ISBN: 9780979366635

Cover picture: "Foot Stool and Books" © 2010
                by Jan L. Coffman

Cover design: H. Ream

Printed in the United States of America

The Columbia Chapter of the Missouri Writers' Guild

The Columbia Chapter of the Missouri Writers' Guild was organized in 1959. Monthly gatherings for members and guests feature critique sessions for poetry and prose and presentations by writing, editing, and publishing professionals. Other activities include an annual conference. Chapter publications include *The Write Stuff,* a quarterly online newsletter for members, and *Well Versed,* the annual literary anthology.

For more information, visit CCMWG's Web site, http://columbiawrites.coin.org.

The Missouri Writers' Guild

The Missouri Writers' Guild was organized in 1915 by Walter Williams, Dean of the School of Journalism at the University of Missouri-Columbia. Membership is open to authors of fiction, nonfiction, scriptwriting, and poetry, whether articles, plays, or books, who have been published for pay. An annual conference features presentations by outstanding national and regional writers, editors, and publishers and cash awards for winners of contests in diverse types of writing.

For more information, visit the Guild's Web site, www.missouriwritersguild.org.

૮૦   ૦૩

Contents

Honorable Mentions: Fiction

Editor's Picks: Nonfiction

Honorable Mentions: Nonfiction

Other Contributions

Photographs

  ℯ ℭ

Appendices

ଚଠ   ଔଓ

We do not write because we want to;
we write because we have to.

-W. Somerset Maugham

Foreword

This Judge's Opinion

Many years ago I interviewed for a managerial position at Hallmark Cards. The interrogation was conducted by a busload of vice presidents of this or that and lasted all day long. In the end, I was turned down. A friend of mine at Hallmark, my personal mole, said the decision came down to a single question:

"Can creativity be taught?"

I said, "No."

Apparently they think it can.

Today I am 65 years old, have published more novels, short stories, personal essays, articles and poems than I can count and know for an absolute fact that Hallmark is wrong.

You can teach spelling, punctuation, sentence structure, paragraph formation, grammar, parts of speech, methodology, technique and so on, and some, through personal example, can even impart a lifelong love for literature, but creativity doesn't come from a classroom, a club or a corporate cubicle-watcher.

It's not transmitted by any person.

It comes from somewhere else, someplace higher: The ceiling, the rooftop, the clouds, the ether, the mysterious dark matter of space or maybe, just maybe, it's a gift from God.

Ancients called it the Muse. Others thanked intoxicants, fairies, ghosts, grandparents and gods of the volcano.

In judging 19 pieces of fiction it became obvious that each was a unique creative expression from a unique creative voice. To discriminate would be a matter of personal taste—hardly fair.

So what's left to judge?

First of all, that which *can* be taught: Structure.

To play the piano you first must learn the keys. To paint like Matisse, Gauguin, Balthus, Monet or van Gogh you must learn shape, color, composition and light. To learn to dance the tango, fandango, foxtrot or waltz you have to watch "Dancing with the Stars," although for this last one there may be better options of which I'm unaware.

I gave each piece a thorough reading and considerable thought. I chose winners because contests require it, but my initial choices were based on the level of structural perfection each piece achieved. Once in a while, however, the creative force was so strong it overshadowed structural failures.

These quickly rose to the top.

If your heart has genuinely been touched in such a way that you can share your thoughts with others then d*** the rules! (Pardon my French.) Anyway, *Tout est bien qui finit bien.*

I hope you enjoy this superb collection as much as I did.

Richard W. Jennings
Overland Park, Kansas
December 2009

ဆ   ﬆ

Preface

Whatever you like to read, the following pages probably include it. We have everything from **A**—"Afternews" to **Z**—"Zoom a Zoom and a Boom Boom."

While most writers stay within their preference in writing, several write both poetry and prose, fiction or nonfiction. Brief biographies show our writers cover the gamut from first-time contributors to authors of multiple books, from Missourians to those who have left the confines of the state borders to live in other areas, be they shore, plains, or mountains. Wherever they are located, they share a love of writing.

Well Versed showcases their work. Many, many thanks to the three judges—Richard W. Jennings, Kenneth (fog) Gilbert, and Susan Satterfield—who donated time to evaluate blind submissions. Outstanding works were selected as Editor's Picks and Honorable Mentions. Approximately two-thirds of the one hundred twenty some submissions were judged ready for publication.

The prizewinning manuscripts appear on the opening pages. Other manuscripts are alphabetized by the authors' names. Photographs by Jan L. Coffman appear throughout the book.

The Columbia Chapter of the Missouri Writers Guild is dedicated to the art and craft of writing. This anthology is one way of providing a venue for those who follow the muse, Erato. More than half of the members submitted manuscripts. Linda Fisher and Eva Ridenour sacrificed many hours of writing time to see through the editing/publication process. I spent computer time putting the manuscripts into book format and doing other "stuff."

Enjoy.

Judy Stock
Managing Editor

ଏ   ଔ

The Guest Editors

Richard W. Jennings, Prose—Fiction

Richard W. Jennings writes novels for young adults and middle-readers and short stories and personal essays for senior adults. He shares his sunlit home in Kansas with three fat brown dachshunds—Milton, Tommy and Danny—and a young *Octopus bimaculoides* named Sandy.

jacob erin-cilberto, Poetry

Also known as Ken "fog" Gilbert, originally from Bronx, New York, now resides in Carbondale, Illinois. erin-cilberto has been writing and publishing poetry since 1970. He currently teaches at John A. Logan and Shawnee Community colleges in Southern Illinois.

His work has appeared in numerous small magazines and journals including: *Café Review*, *Skyline Magazine*, *Hudson View*, *Wind Journal*, *Pegasus*, *Parnassus* and others. erin-cilberto also writes reviews of poetry books for *Chiron Review*, *Skyline Review* and others. He has reviewed books by B. Z. Niditch, musician Tom Maclear and others. His eleventh and newest book of poetry, *An Abstract Waltz*, is scheduled for release this December. erin-cilberto has been nominated for a Pushcart Prize in Poetry in 2006-2008. He also teaches poetry workshops for Heartland Writers Guild, Southern Illinois Writers Guild and Union County Writers Guild.

Susan Satterfield, Prose—Nonfiction

Susan Satterfield is the author of a number of published short stories including "Mirror of His Soul" and "The Changing," appearing in *Eldritch Tales*, and "A Perfect World," appearing in the Yard Dog Press anthology, *Stories That Won't Make Your Parents Hurl*. Her chapbook, *Mirror Images*, was published by Yard Dog Press in May of 2002. "The Lady Killer" and "Sweet Teddy" appeared in an anthology entitled *Small Bites*, which was a benefit for author, Charles Grant. She is also the author of "A Bubba Poet" found in *The International House of Bubbas* and "What Goes Around" from the anthology *Flush Fiction*. Susan's seventh short story entitled, "Close Encounters of the Bubba Kind," can be found in the Yard Dog Press anthology *Houston, We've Got Bubbas*. Her latest sale is a poem entitled "The Hunger: A Zombie Poem," which appeared in October 2009 in an anthology titled *Vicious Verses and Reanimated Rhyme* from Costcom Entertainment. She has a number of writing projects on (and sometimes under) the table.

Susan is an English Instructor at Metropolitan Community College-Longview in Lee's Summit, Missouri, where she is founder and has been the coordinator for the MCC-Longview Literary Festival the past two years. She lives in Lee's Summit with her extended family including four dogs, four cats, and assorted fish.

80 ∞ 03

Editors' Picks
and
Honorable Mentions

Jan L. Coffman

Dear Editor

    ≔   ≓

Editor's Picks: Poetry

Martin Turner

Afternews

Hearing that cherry blossoms
    are opening together
    across an ocean
    this year
I cried for the one who
    told how quickly
    today's bomb
    made empty places
    in the shape of loved ones

ᛞ   ᚳ

C. B. O'Brien

The Sculptor

His work is deconstruction; his heart
(a stone hope pounding where his hands are)
beats the vision of his quarry clear.
Hammer and point command the hapless mass
that smiled in the sun for a million years,
proud in her totality.
His passion compels her limited flesh,
pressing out the vintage spirit,
leaving the bitter rape
emptied on her adamantine pedestal:
mother, daughter, wife;
the world orbiting her frozen pirouette.
Her whispering, polished lips a plea;
her long Cytherean arms
in their gentlest inquiring curve;
narrow fingers lifting a furtive prayer—
a call to join her
in a kind of godly meld,
to fill the voids of her defilement
and somehow make her whole again.

⁎♹⁏

Honorable Mentions: Poetry

J. M. Brandt

Become Uneven
  —to R. Chownyk

each promise is different
metal, different weight. my
hands on the lathe.

with my blood, I've already
signed each promise,
even when I can't

quite cut or make the
shape that I wanted or
possibly needed.

edges become uneven.
metal splinters. hours wasted.
the sounds of breaking.

ᛒᚖ   ᚽᛒ

C. B. O'Brien

The Wall

Up from the cold collusion of the bloodless years
a pale hand rises, coupling with the black slab
in a sort of sad consortium;
finding the mark; the name;
the lie, caressing the ridges and valleys of the wound
as if they held a life reduced—
the man her boy would be in another world—
a world without a wall.
Patrolling the curves and angles
of the scar, she searches for the soul
in their geometry.
And fifty thousand names
await their fifty thousand hands;
wait on this graven horizontal totem;
stretched out like a dead soldier.

༄   ༅

Martin Turner

Rural Route

The mailbox crop
   looks bad
After people go
   they stay awhile
Battered soon by snowplows
   that grope at night
Along the twisting blacktop
   with no lines

৪০ come

Jan L Coffman

The Right Pen

Editor's Picks: Fiction

Linda Fisher

The Road Trip

Amanda and Lily's first road trip was also Henry's last. Henry was in a small plastic box tucked securely into the trunk of his 1975 Corvette convertible. The two fifty-five-year-old women hadn't planned on taking Henry's ashes to the Big Thompson River, but he had always been inconsiderate.

Lily had briefly been married to Henry until he abandoned her for a younger, prettier woman. The red Corvette had been his chick magnet soon after their divorce.

After Lily and Henry parted ways, he married and divorced three other women, and not always in the proper order. He had gotten in a bit of a hurry and married wife #3 before divorcing wife #2. Lust and liquor were to blame for his error in judgment. Neither woman had seen the humor in the situation.

"Don't you cry any tears over that good-for-nothin' man," Amanda said as she steered the car into a McDonald's parking lot. She patted Lily's hand. "I'm doing this for you, Lily, not for Henry." The wind whipped Amanda's strawberry hair around her face. Leaving the top down seemed like a great idea early this morning, but the Kansas wind was hot and the sun barreled down. Her fair skin felt tight and had turned a pinkish color.

Lily wiped her eyes with the back of her hand. "I loved him at one time, and now I feel bad that I'm not even sad he's gone."

"Then why the tears? After all, he was my brother-in-law and I'm not crying." Thank goodness Amanda's belated husband had not shared many traits with his brother.

Lily shrugged. "I'm tender hearted, I guess."

"That's the truth! Not many ex-wives would have stayed by him once he was sick. His latest main squeeze certainly bailed in a hurry."

"Don't you think it's sad that no one cares he's gone? Doesn't it just break your heart to think that he asked us to spread his ashes?" Lily adjusted her sunglasses on her nose and tightened the scarf covering her dark curly hair.

"No, I'm just mad the old fool asked us to do this. I'm going to miss bunko this week," Amanda said. She looked at the map. "Let's stay at Colby, Kansas, tonight and go on to Colorado in the morning?"

Before they left McDonald's, they put the top up on the convertible. Lily groused about how impractical the car was, and how inappropriate for carrying human remains.

After the long day of driving, the two had fallen silent by the time they reached Colby. They began to unload their suitcases at Day's Inn. Lily picked up the box with Henry's ashes.

"For Christ's sake, don't tell me you plan on taking those things into the room!" Amanda spat out the words.

"It doesn't seem proper to leave Henry in the car," Lily said.

"Like he knows or cares what we do. We should have dumped the ashes into the pond and been done with it."

Lily straightened her shoulders. "I gave him my word," she said.

Daylight found the two women on Interstate 70 headed toward Henry's final destination. After consulting their Rand McNally, they decided to go through Loveland and down Highway 34 toward Estes Park. Along the route, they would find an appropriate spot to scatter the ashes.

They stopped at Safeway and bought bologna, cheese, bread, and Fritos for a picnic lunch. They drove beside the breathtaking Big Thompson and stopped at a roadside area to eat.

"Shall we scatter the ashes here?" Amanda asked.

"I don't think this is a good spot," said Lily.

"Looks as good as any to me," said Amanda. "Besides, once we get rid of the ashes, we can enjoy our little road trip."

"It just doesn't seem right," said Lily. "I mean, after all, this should be a solemn occasion and done with dignity."

"I say it just needs to be done." Amanda gathered up the picnic remains and stuffed them back into the cooler. She was half tempted to grab the box and shake the ashes into the running water below. Instead, she set the box aside and shoved the cooler back into the trunk.

As she pulled back onto the highway, she said, "Let me know when you find the perfect spot."

They rode in silence. Amanda pulled off in scenic spot after scenic spot. Lily would shake her head. The areas just didn't seem right to fulfill her solemn duty to Henry.

"Let's go into Estes and look for a place on the way back," said Lily.

"You mean we're just going to tool around town with Henry in the trunk?" asked Amanda.

"He isn't hurting anything. I don't want to scatter his ashes in the wrong spot."

They drove into Estes Park and checked into the Comfort Inn. They opened the trunk and started to remove their luggage.

"Oh, my goodness, sakes alive!" shrieked Lily. "Where is Henry?"

"Quit that carrying on," scolded Amanda. "He's right there behind the cooler . . ." Her voice trailed off as she shoved the cooler aside to find no box. Then, she remembered setting the box on the ground when she put the cooler in the trunk.

"Uh, I think I might have left the box at the overlook where we had lunch," Amanda admitted.

"We have to drive back up there and get Henry," Lily said.

"We better wait until morning," said Amanda. "I don't think we could find it in the dark."

"This is awful," Lily said. She began to bawl. Her shoulders heaved and her nose began to drip.

Amanda handed her a handkerchief. "It will be all right," she said in as soothing a tone as she could muster. "The box will be there. After all, who would take a box of ashes?"

At Lily's insistence they were up early. Amanda ate waffles, but Lily only had black coffee. She was nervous and upset about leaving poor Henry alongside the highway overnight. Amanda couldn't figure out what the big deal was—roadside area or river bottom, who really cared?

They drove back up the Big Thompson and found the roadside scenic area. Casually, they walked to the edge of the lot to look at the river flowing below.

"I don't see Henry," whispered Lily.

"Of course, you don't," said Amanda. "That conversion van is parked where we were so it has to be behind it."

Three little boys came screaming past Amanda and Lily. They stopped to throw rocks into the river. Their parents occasionally urged the boys to be careful.

The mother called the kids to the van to eat. Amanda pulled out a camera and began to take pictures. The family probably wondered why the two women just kept hanging around.

The kids finished eating and Mom began to put things away while Dad walked to the overlook to smoke a cigarette.

Amanda and Lily kept casting their eyes in the direction of the family willing them to leave so they could retrieve Henry.

"Look, Daddy!" shouted one of the boys. "See how good I can throw!"

Lily looked in his direction just in time to see him heave a small plastic box into the water far below. She covered her mouth to stifle a scream.

"What the heck was that?" his dad asked.

"Just a box of sand," he said.

"Time to go!" Mom yelled. The kids ran giggling toward the van.

Amanda and Lily walked to the railing and peered into the rushing water below. They could not see the plastic box.

"What do we do now?" asked Lily.

"Oh, for Pete's sake," said Amanda. "The ashes are in the Big Thompson just like the old coot wanted. You've done your duty by him."

"Henry didn't want to be tossed in like that—still in the box."

"What difference does it make? Did he say to take him out of the box?" Amanda asked.

"He said, 'Put my ashes in the Big Thompson,' but I know he didn't want some show-off kid to throw him in box and all," said Lily.

"Lily, didn't that little kid remind you of someone?"

"Yes, he did, come to think of it. He looked a lot like Henry, didn't he?"

"You know, Lily, the Lord works in mysterious ways. You couldn't seem to let go of the ashes, so it was taken out of your hands."

Mulling over that possibility, they climbed into the car. "Let's go back to Estes," said Lily. "I've always wanted to ride that Aerial Tramway." She smiled and removed her scarf, letting the wind ruffle her hair.

Neither woman noticed the box sitting near the edge of the weeds. It was nearly identical to the one filled with sand that the boy had heaved into the water. Lily would have been appalled had she known they abandoned Henry's ashes like trash beside the road, but Amanda would have been amused.

ಬ ಔ

Honorable Mentions: Fiction

Lar Glendal Wallace

The Lesson

Today would be my last day of working here in Omaha and I was looking forward to returning home to my family in Columbia, Missouri. I arrived to my final substitute teaching assignment for the Omaha Public Schools with my usual sense of challenge in an attempt to touch the life of a child or older student. Upon entering Horace Mann Magnet Center, I was greeted with the delightful sounds of waltz and chamber music, bright patchwork flooring, and nickel-plated lighting fixtures. Dazzling earth tone colors were everywhere. The entrance murals. The office corridors. The bulletin boards. The classrooms. Everywhere.

No bells rang in the school's energetic hallways. The kids just walked out of class when "it was time." Mann was 85% Hispanic in enrollment, and in the halls you saw and heard a microcosmic Spanish-speaking world of scurrying 5th through 8th graders, all excited to be living and laughing in their own right. From the state-of-the-art library center to the wire-strung stairways, the school resembled an enchanted spread of contemporary design with an edgy splendor. This was not a regular-looking school. It was a new age, interactive, scholastic museum. In short, it looked like Ty Pennington and his team were hired as the contractual decorators. I felt like a child myself.

According to the lesson plans, I was assigned to work in an ESL class with five Spanish-speaking students in the morning session and nineteen Spanish kids and one African student in the afternoon session. The classroom was all aglow with harvest colored pendant chandeliers and shiny oak veneer shelving. After my formal introduction with the students about the lesson plans, they moved to their assigned workstations.

Ten minutes later, Al Delgado, my teacher assistant, walked in the classroom. Fully-gray haired, bespectacled in large wire frames, he wore a long, thick, serpentine gold chain with a shiny, gold key chain around his neck. Dressed in black cowboy boots with gold wing tips (the shape of a horseshoe), black jeans and wearing a white Mann school t-shirt, Mr. Delgado looked like an unassuming motorcycle gang president. Yet, his dark, keen eyes and slow gait emitted an unspoken grace and richness. A sense of settled peace that came from paying your dues in this life. His smile revealed an amazing rapport with kids that worked like magic. He went immediately over to their desks and mumbled a few Spanish words of social greeting. He knew their language. He knew their habits. It was as if he knew how these energy-sprung middle-schoolers "operated." He could have easily been a guidance counselor or school psychologist—but in stark reality, he was already that and more.

I was sitting at the teacher's desk when Mr. Delgado walked over to me. He spoke with a hip, yet warmly dignified, presence, "Howyadoin?"

Mr. Delgado was a born-again, street-savvy griot. A former cop, Vietnam vet, and Juvenile Center counselor, he arrived in this country illegally in 1963 from Mexico City where he was a certificated classroom teacher. Sometime back he married, had children, had other women and "lived the life" until one day he found himself pacing his living room floor with a bottle of prescription pills in his hand because his life "was a mess." He started crying and told God that if he "turned his life around" he would change. That next morning started the first real day of the rest of his "sweet life." He started going to church and soon prayed for a young, beautiful, clean and Christian wife.

"I did have a long list for God." He smiled.

He went on to say that one day a lady from a cleaning service came to his apartment and they blended immediately. She was everything he had hoped for. The rest is history. Three months later they married. He never as much as kissed her before their wedding day. She had two young sons, one of whom, now fourteen, threatened to kill him if he came near "their house." So Mr. Delgado and his wife lived on opposite sides of town in Omaha for many years. He lived in a secluded house off 24th Street and his wife stayed clear across town in an area called Bellevue. But she managed to come over to his house every morning at seven and they would spend time together "that way." For now it worked.

As he talked about this part of his life, I could see that he truly loved his wife and wanted totally what was best for everybody. Even if it hurt him. His voice started to rumble and tremble at the same time. He paused. I looked away at the students who were now working independently on a geography lesson. He started to speak a little softer. I smiled.

"Would you . . . like to be ex . . .?" I hesitated, sensing that he was a man quite capable of knowing whether or not he needed to excuse himself.

"It's fine." He politely interrupted. I could see that it was. The classroom, the five students, the aura around him, us, our conversation. Everything.

"How long have you lived here?" I asked.

"I moved here two years ago from Center Springs, Tulsa. I worked as a Juvenile Center officer. I told myself . . . I was seeing all these Hispanic kids. Kids from the barrios where I grew up. All being put in prison and I thought to myself, if I could reach them before they get here then that would be better."

I pranced over to the five students who were now watching a Spanish history video lesson on their assigned computer.

"You guys have any questions about the lesson?"

"No, Ms. Teacher. We always know what to do." A pudgy, slightly attractive female student spoke for the group.

I was not used to this kind of classroom engagement. I was used to dodging spitballs, catching paper balls and monitoring cell phone usage from sassy-mouthed teens. But these students were all smiles and working on task. I observed for a few minutes then scurried back to my desk.

". . . so, I came to the schools. That's where the need is. Here. I love my job and I love these kids. They respect me and know I understand them and where they come from. I grew up hard myself. But now through God, I have a better life . . . a sweet life," Mr. Delgado continued.

"I have a wife, a good job, and a family. I even teach English to the elderly Spanish people here and to the young Spanish kids in the area. After twelve years of prayer, I have finally been able to see my own kids. Now being here in Omaha, I know I make a difference by reaching just one child at a time. Just one. Only one at a time is all it takes. You might not see results right away but keep living . . . you will. The Word says, *One plants, another waters, but God gives the increase.* So don't worry about it, just do your part. Just do your part. It may be years and years before you see results, but they will turn around. That kid you talked to will turn around. I see it all the time in my own life."

His voice got sterner. "Listen. This one kid I had in the juvenile center saw me about five years ago and came up to me and said, 'You're the reason I got my life together. It's what you said to me.'"

Suddenly my body jolted. The next thing I knew, I had jumped up and walked across the room to find the tissue box because my mascara was burning something fierce. As I stumbled away, a couple of impatiently waiting tears rolled down my face . . .

It has been over two years since I left Omaha. I now realize that the lesson that day came from Mr. Delgado and the delightful class of students from my ESL teaching assignment. The real lesson was the growth of my perception and appreciation of other voices and other cultures. On that day, my final day in that classroom—life wasn't about me trying to be the master teacher or giving the lesson. No, life in that moment was the lesson I had received.

৪ৎ ৎঙ

Teresa Shields Parker

The Splinter

In a dirt pile, at the edge of the playground, she sits, bits and pieces of stuff piled to her side. She must dig with her hands to find the other pieces, for they are buried. Gently she removes the dirt like an archeologist uncovering a find. When she finds a piece, she claps her hands in joy and carefully places it in her special pile. The pile is small, just fragments and pieces of commonly found items that would need to be pieced together if they were ever to resemble what they once were. The going is slow because some pieces are buried deep. Getting up, she dusts off her light pink dress, tossing her white sweater on the ground near her socks and shoes. She skips to the nearby trees now green with tiny buds appearing and begins to search for something. With an, "Aha," she picks up a stick and then an old soda can and gleefully returns to the dirt pile to continue digging.

The lady with baggy, gray pants walks with the aid of a cane. She slowly makes her way to a nearby wooden park bench. She pulls her black coat tighter around her frail body. She lowers herself carefully to the bench. She wishes she'd remembered to wear her gloves when she notices the jagged wooden edges and reminds herself not to run along them with her hand for fear of splinters. They do hurt something awful and with her arthritis, splinters are impossible for her to remove. Once she had one that became infected. She didn't have money for the doctor and the little thing nearly killed her. She worked at it until it finally came out, but it was a long time coming. No, avoiding splinters was definitely the best choice.

It is a spring day but a brisk breeze is blowing. Her ears are cold and she can't afford to be sick again. From her pocket, she pulls a scarf. Its faint purple and red flowers blow in the breeze.

She wrestles it from the wind, folds it into a triangle, places it over her head and ties it around her chin. She watches the little girl as she continues her digging. With each item the child finds, her entire face lights up with the wonderment of discovery. She lifts her face to the sun and giggles as only little girls do. The lady adjusts her scarf, sits back, closes her eyes, and turns her face to the warmth of the sun and leans her head against the back of the wooden park bench.

Suddenly, the little girl shrieks with delight and holds up a small piece of wood. She turns, sees the lady, looks at the piece again, then with understanding in her eyes, runs to her.

"Lady, Lady," she says, tugging at her coat. "Lady, Lady, wake up."

The lady slowly raises her head and looks at the girl's dress blowing in the breeze, blonde bangs falling across her eyes, bare toes wriggling in the grass.

"I have a part of you," she says holding out the small wooden sliver.

"A part of me?"

"Yes, it is a part of you and you must have it." She places the piece in the lady's hand and runs back to the dirt pile, digging more furiously.

"Girl, Girl," the lady calls.

The girl puts down her tools and runs back to the bench.

"What is this?"

"It is a splinter."

"A splinter is not part of me. You are crazy. Why would I want this?"

"I'm not sure. Maybe a small problem will keep you from having a bigger one?"

"Look, splinters hurt and I have arthritis. I can't remove them and if I can't remove them, they become bigger problems. I don't want this."

"There is another part to it; I just haven't found it yet. When I do, I'll bring it to you. It will make sense then." She smiles as the lady stares at the wooden sliver.

"I could throw it away," the lady says.

"No, it is part of you. You cannot throw it away."

"Why do I need it?"

"You need it to be whole."

"But it will hurt."

"Then you must go through the pain." Her innocent eyes lock with the lady's experienced ones and hold her gaze for what seems like an eternity.

The lady shakes her head. She is familiar with pain in her life. "It will cause infection. I will not be able to remove it by myself and I have no money for a doctor."

The girl pats the wrinkled hand. "I will find the other part." With that, she runs back to the dirt pile.

The lady looks at the piece of wood, shivers, pulls her coat tighter around her and sighs. From her pocket, she takes a handkerchief with a pink flower embroidered in the corner. She carefully wraps the wooden sliver and holds it in her hand.

The blonde-haired girl is digging furiously now. Though she finds various things, she shakes her head at each discovery and places it in her special pile.

The lady has her eyes closed again, head laid back against the bench, eyes lifted upward to the sun once again. Her coat has gapped open again, but the sun is shining brightly.

"Yes," the girl shouts. "Yes. I found it."

Grasping the small object she runs back to the bench.

"Lady, Lady, I found it."

The lady raises her head to look in the little girl's bright, blue eyes now wide with excitement. With gusto, the girl thrusts the piece toward the reticent lady.

"It will help you with the sliver."

The lady carefully places the handkerchief, which she still holds in her hand in her pocket. She opens her hand to receive the girl's gift.

"Why this is nothing more than a common, ordinary straight pin," she says.

"No, it is *the* pin that will remove your sliver when it becomes a splinter," the little girl explains. "It is what you need to survive the splinter. It is necessary."

"But this sliver will not become a splinter if I simply throw it away."

"You cannot. It is part of you. You must experience this little pain now. See, He's even giving you the way to remove it. A small pain now may keep you from a bigger sorrow later. It is part of the plan. It is part of what will make you whole."

"What plan?"

"His plan."

"His plan is not a very good one then. I think I can make a better plan than that."

The lady attempts to laugh, but it comes out as more of a cough. She pulls the handkerchief from her pocket, finds the small wooden sliver and lays it on the bench. She folds the handkerchief and puts in back in her pocket.

"Please, you must take it, or His plan will not work and . . . "

". . . And what? Will the sun refuse to shine? The moon turn to blood?" Her voice seems to contain all the cynicism of those throughout the ages who had been offered the choice but had refused to take it.

Tears form in the girl's eyes when the lady lays the pin on the bench, as well. Because the lady is a little unsteady, she uses her hands to push off the bench as she stands to grab her cane, leaning slightly on the bench before she begins to walk. When she puts her hands on the bench, the sliver imbeds itself in her hand. She feels a little twinge, but thinks nothing of it. She leans against the bench to steady herself. The pin falls through the wooden slats of the bench to the weeds below and bounces into a crack in the ground.

The girl in the pink dress knows many things. Instantly, she knows the sliver has imbedded itself in the lady and the pin has been lost forever in the earth. Now, the thing designed to remove the splinter is gone, lost to the lady in the black coat.

The girl watches the lady walk away leaning a little more heavily on the cane. The lady stops and rubs a spot on her hand, then slowly continues on her journey. She turns back to the little girl, laughs a low cackling laugh, shakes her head and walks on.

Silently, the girl's tears fall on the ground beneath the bench watering the weeds and the cracked, dry ground.

৪০   ৪৩

Linda Fisher

The Storm of Last Chance

Dasha twisted her auburn hair into a knot on the top of her head to keep it from sticking to her neck. She sprawled on the porch swing of the Kansas farmhouse, brooding. Although it was almost noon, she wore only a thin cotton nightgown. She pushed against the paint peeled boards with one bare foot and used the momentum of the swing to stir up a breeze.

Logan deserted her this morning, the back of the pickup heaped with his belongings. He even took the beagle, Shorty. Said he couldn't depend on her to take proper care of Shorty since she could not take care of herself.

He had threatened to leave for the past six months. "Dasha, you need to stop drinking. Promise you will."

Dasha glared at him with whiskey-bleared eyes and said, "You know I never make promises I can't keep." She may be a drunk, or alcoholic, but Dasha prided herself on her honesty.

"I've had it," he said. Those simple words summed up twenty years of hurt, anger, disappointment. His shoulders slumped and he looked defeated. Dasha pitied him. She felt bad for the rip in his jeans, his scuffed boots, his battered Stetson. Maybe he would find a woman who was younger, prettier, and sober.

She lifted the bottle to her lips and took an unladylike swig of Southern Comfort. Black clouds loomed in the southwest, promising rain for the parched lawn and a dust settling for the dirt road. Dust hovered over the house like a mist although an hour had passed since Logan drove down the lane and headed east on the highway.

Dasha couldn't remember when the bottle became her solace, a replacement for love. She had given up on life after the miscarriage, a son that was not to be. Then Logan gave up on her.

Ahead of the storm front, sighs of a southern breeze clanged the wind chimes reminding Dasha of how Logan had picked her up so she could hang them. "A storm's brewin'," she said aloud. She didn't even have Shorty to talk to now.

Lost in thought, Dasha stared at the impending storm but did not see it. The swirling clouds, streaks of lightening and thunder grumblings became backdrops to the drama in her head—Logan's laugh, his rough hands clutching hers, his strong arms wrapped around her, the heat that breathed through her at his touch. Logan had been her leading man since she was sixteen years old.

Hailstones pelted the house, but Dasha, sheltered by the porch, ignored the ominous flat hail and its implications. The wind shifted directions, and she shivered from the sudden cold draft. She took another drink. The rumble in the distance sounded like large earth-moving equipment. Dasha closed her eyes. Her limbs felt heavy, unresponsive, but the numbing effect of the liquor did not dull the ache of losing Logan—and Shorty.

The funnel dropped from the clouds kicking up dirt and debris. Dasha slipped into another world, another time. Logan's dad played the fiddle and his uncle strummed his Gibson guitar. Dasha danced with Logan and he whirled her around and around making her dizzy, but so lighthearted she felt she could float like fluffy clouds.

Caught up in reminiscing, Dasha dozed. Last night had been so traumatic she had not slept.

The old Ford bounced over the potholes in the lane. A box of tools fell off the back of the truck and thudded unheeded into the road. The pickup screeched to a halt. Shorty bounded out of the open truck window outpacing Logan in a race toward Dasha.

"Dasha, we need to get to the cellar! The storm is headed this way."

Dasha forced her puffy eyes open. "Why do you care? You could have been out of the county by now."

"Darn it, Dasha. I felt like I'd left part of me behind. I was on my way back when I saw the tornado."

"Tornado?" Dasha's eyes bulged, the alcohol induced lethargy replaced with heart-pounding panic. Since a childhood friend had been killed by a tornado, Dasha had an unreasonable fear of storms. The only time she felt safe was when Logan held her in his arms.

The suffocating air was dark and heavy, black with flying debris. Logan shouted over the roaring wind, "Come on, Dasha. We have to go *now*!"

Logan wrapped an arm around Dasha's shoulders and they bent into the cyclonic gale, into a darkness like the end of the world. Dasha's legs shook from fear and too much liquor. She collapsed to the ground while Logan tugged open the heavy cellar door. Shorty raced down the steps.

The pickup lifted into the air and they heard a boom as it slammed cab first into the garden. Boxes, clothing, fishing tackle, a dirt bike, all so carefully loaded into the bed of the pickup last night were sucked up into the funnel. A power pole snapped in pieces, the crossarms dangled from the power lines. The storm stripped siding and shingles from the house. The porch collapsed, smashing the swing and potted geraniums.

Shorty ran from the cellar and howled as he cowered against Dasha where she lay on the ground. Logan pulled Dasha to her feet, she reached out to steady herself against the bucking wind, and saw the bottle of Southern Comfort clutched in her hand. With Logan's arm around her, the tornado bearing down on them, she flung the bottle into the darkness. She picked up Shorty and walked steadily down the steps into the cellar.

She and Logan crouched in the dark, his arms wrapped tightly around her. "I promise you—I will never drink again," she said. This was her last chance with Logan. She felt stronger and more hopeful than she had in years and no longer feared the storm.

ಏ   ಛ

Jan L. Coffman

Post Cards

ജ   ങ

Editor's Picks: Nonfiction

Cate Richard

Gift From the Sea

Sometimes a place calls to you before you even know it exists. Sometimes the reasons for this sneak up on you like a summer thunderstorm, turning an otherwise tropical depression day into a pleasant afternoon delight. Sometimes they turn out to be more than an interlude; they offer a new perspective on life gone wrong, putting hope in a place you thought it might never live again. Milton called them "everyday epiphanies . . . transcendent moments of awe that change forever how we view life and the world."

I wasn't expecting epiphanies when my friend asked me to join her and her dad on a trip to a kidney-shaped island named Sanibel and her appendix sister Captiva off Florida's Gulf coast. The only thing I knew about the place was that Cynthia loved it and visited every year. Having grown up near Galveston, the heat and humidity on an organ-shaped island in July wasn't my first choice for a getaway. But being offered a place to stay for a week for the price of a plane ticket wasn't a trip to be turned down—especially if you'd just been through a divorce and needed a fresh look at life. I said 'yes' and packed my bags.

The last thing I threw into my carry-on was a copy of Anne Morrow Lindbergh's *Gift from the Sea*. I hadn't read the book in ages, so opening it on the plane I was surprised to see the inscription, written by another friend who'd given it to me after a trip to San Diego almost fifteen years earlier. Fond memories came to mind, the blue water of the Pacific, swirls of life in tide pools at La Joya, graceful strides of dolphins beyond the cliffs at Del Mar, laughs and cups of tea with my friend. All gifts from the sea, now sparkling jewels of memory. Then that image faded, replaced by the bittersweet recollection of another love lost, another door closed, another divorce. *Why can't I ever get it right*? I wondered, thinking about how, in *this* marriage, I thought I had. Banishing the question, I told myself I wasn't flying halfway across the country to dwell on problems I could think about at home. I returned to the book, and read about AML's shells for the rest of the plane ride.

Something about visiting a new place calls to mind life's infinite possibilities, no matter what may have happened to convince you none exist. I remembered this as soon as I stepped into the Florida sunshine. I remembered as long as I had breath in my body, things could get better. Still skeptical about *how* much better, anything would be an improvement over the past lonely year. After all, life goes on even when you don't particularly want it to.

Turns out Sanibel had plenty of surprises, if not epiphanies. I hadn't expected a marshy alligator-infested swamp, yet parts of it *are* marshy, alligator-infested, and swampy. Other parts are just beach. The strange looking mangrove trees intrigued me most, their exposed roots grasping through seawater like slender fingers seeking something solid to latch on to. Wasn't that what we all wanted from life, something solid to hold on to? Just when I thought I'd found it, here I was back in the swamp, sinking, trying to gather up pieces of a broken life and get hold of 'me' again. What was it AML wrote?—All you have to do is "wait for a gift from the sea." What little hope I had bade me wait. Besides, if a gift from the sea were to show up anywhere, Sanibel had an edge, its nickname being "Shell Island."

So within minutes of arrival and minor prodding from me, we donned our sun protection gear and hit the shore. When you first get to the beach, all you want to do is stand at the water's edge, soak in the sun and sound of the waves, and drown in utter calm. Time stops, and nothing and nowhere are more important than this moment. I held that pause until my stresses melted away. Then I started hunting for shells. Unfortunately, the caliber of the shells offered little to impress—tiny, broken, boring, nothing like those AML described in her book. Disappointment enveloped me like an unwelcome houseguest. Uncharacteristically, I told it to take a hike. So what if I didn't see any cool shells today; I had a week to find my gift. I held on to Emily Dickenson's hope, that "thing with feathers that perches in your soul and sings the tune without the words and never stops at all." I held on.

Turns out I was nowhere near the ocean when I got my first gift. I found it on a shelf in a little island shop, a small blue revised version of *Gift from the Sea*. When I saw it, somehow I *knew*. Anne Morrow Lindbergh wrote that book *here*. Not exactly here, but close enough.

Remember that little appendix sister just to the north? Little nine-mile long Captiva? *That's* where she found the shells called whelks, argonauta, double sunrise; *that's* where she wrote that wonderful memoir women everywhere have cherished for over fifty years, because it gave us permission to take time for ourselves, to find out who we are, to go to islands on our own, to pick up shells and listen to what they're trying to tell us about life. Just up the road, she found *her* gifts from the sea. All I had to do now was find mine.

And I did. It just took time . . . and small disappointments—a million broken boring shells on the beach, finding Captiva no longer charming and isolated but over-grown with gaudy mansions and touristy venues. But other gifts showed up: the laughter of friends, companionship over good food and wine, refreshing bike rides through mangrove-shaded parks, sunlight on the sea, glimpses of thick-shelled tortoises plodding like they had somewhere important to go and couldn't be delayed by clumsiness or lack of options—and did I say it already?—

laughter with friends. I started to believe someday I might feel happy again. Then I found the real reason the island had called me.

Walking along the beach one evening, I decided even though I still wanted my gift from the sea, I could live without it. I was learning I could live without a lot of things. Or maybe I was simply letting go of hope. Still, making one last-ditch effort, I called an intention, *wouldn't it be nice if I found a gift from the sea*?

Stepping forward, a shadow beneath the waves caught my eye then magically it appeared—a whelk! Not a big one, only about four inches, but to me perfect as a newborn—brown striped, beautiful round head, straight delicate point at the end, no living creature inside! (Those must return to *their* watery homes but this one I could keep in *my* own!)

Sending silent thanks to the Universe, I took a couple more steps then stumbled upon the Mother Lode. Astounded, at my feet lay a pile of fifteen or twenty Florida fighting conches (orange and white, similar to a whelk but squattier and thicker-skinned) and eight to ten, four to five inch across, perfectly symmetrical *sand dollars*! I felt like a pirate stumbling on buried treasure that wasn't buried any more—all I had to do was reach down and pick it up. I gently—albeit greedily—grabbed as many shells as I could while screaming 'Thank You!' to the gods of the sea.

But after a moment or two, I stepped back, drew a calming breath, and reprimanded my pirate self. How many shells did I really need? I might not even be able to get the delicate sand dollars home without breaking them. I selected a few and left the others for the next seeker.

I stared at that pile of shells for a long time. I thought about how small and limited my life had felt recently, and how simply discovering one beautiful brown whelk meant so much. Just one perfect specimen of promise, reminding me there were still good things to find. I was happy with my gift, and it would have been enough. But the sea hadn't finished giving. She wanted me to remember if I just kept going, I'd find more. I would always find more, because the only person placing limits on how much I could have was *me*. Sanibel called me here to learn *this*. To reassure me there would always be not just enough, but *more* than enough. Didn't Anne say it so well at the end of her book—"There are other beaches to explore. There are more shells to find. This is only a beginning."

Hope restored, I retreated from the shells and made my way back toward the *real* gifts I'd received from my time by the sea. Did I mention the laughter of friends?

Cate Richard

Mermaid

ᚄ   ᚉ

Ida Bettis Fogle

Deena

Deena introduced me to Ramadan and romance novels on the same day. I offered her some of my lunch when I noticed she didn't have any. She declined, explaining to me about the Muslim holiday time during which they fasted throughout the daylight hours. Then she went back to reading *The Secret of the Glen* by Barbara Cartland, looking up after a few minutes to say, "You should read this book. It's really good."

This was during my first year of junior high, that world in which conformity was more important than it ever had been in, oh, a convent, or one of Mao's re-education camps. Deena and I met in gym class, and formed a bond as the only two girls not wearing the standard gym uniform. Neither of us was allowed to wear shorts, a restriction that made me feel I was dying inside a little each P.E. day.

I already bore the affliction of hair that wouldn't feather, growing in thick, frizzy corkscrews as it did. This would have been acceptable, I suppose, had my skin been darker. But a white girl, one who flushed pink with the slightest change in temperature, with nappy hair? Nappy blonde hair? It just wasn't done. Even one of my African American classmates eventually took it upon herself to enlighten me about the existence of something called hair relaxer. Then there was my name, my old patchwork granny name, one you'd never find attached to a cheerleader with stylable hair. So with those burdens weighing on me, I felt certain the sweatpants-in-lieu-of-shorts would be the last trowel full of cement hardening on my feet as I plunged to the bottom, under the crushing waters of junior high.

But then Deena appeared, also not in shorts. As time went on, we discovered more we had in common. We were both voracious readers and both came from large families. But the characteristics that brought us closest were the ones that set us apart from the other students, the things we didn't do, mostly. "You've never seen *Saturday Night Live*? Neither have I! You won't be allowed to go to school dances? Same here!"

I thought of it as a sort of support group: Outsiders Living with Unusual Parental Restrictions United. We stuck together at school much as teens with diabetes might eat lunch together. Because who else would understand? Or kids with other disabilities—shriveled thalidomide arms perhaps—would give each other knowing looks, looks saying, "Those people with two functional hands just don't get it. But We—We understand each other, as we endure the same hardships. Not that we would have chosen this for ourselves, but there it is anyway. What are you going to do?"

Part of my survival technique involved adopting an air of superiority, affecting the righteous strength of those who have suffered, the toughness of the ascetic living in the mountain cave, existing on berries, an existence your soft, common person couldn't endure. All the same, I was unspeakably grateful not to be in the cave alone.

When Richard Berkely ran for the office of Mayor of Kansas City against Bruce Watkins in a highly charged campaign, Deena and I discussed it with rolled eyes, the same way we talked about everything that involved our parents.

"What do you mean, who is my dad supporting?" she asked. "Berkely is Jewish. My father says we'll move out of the city if he's elected. Don't know about my mom, though. What about your parents?"

"You think my dad would ever vote for anyone but the white guy?" I said as if she actually knew my dad, as if she had lived with him like I had. "But my mother . . . I'm not sure."

Our mothers were both more progressive than their husbands, though our respective fathers seemed to be less aware of it than we were. I'm pretty sure my friend Deena knew more about my mother's voting record than my dad did.

I never set foot in Deena's house and she never came to mine. But as we traded stories I felt I knew her family members; they sounded so much like mine. Our fathers were steadfast in their beliefs, certain they already knew what they needed to know, and largely unaware of the happenings within their own families. Mine never knew his youngest daughter's most constant companion at school was a foreigner (originally from Jordan) and a Muslim. Deena's father never realized his daughter had struck up a friendship with someone from a family of the fundamentalist Christian persuasion.

Deena didn't wear a head covering of any kind. In fact, she dressed pretty much as I did: jeans and t-shirts (not too tight) in the summer, jeans and sweatshirts in the winter. Nothing above the knee, no spaghetti-strap shirts, no bathing suits. Ever. You wouldn't immediately spot her as the Muslim girl, as far as I know the only one in the entire school. Whether her short sleeves and lack of hair cover indicated an unusual liberalism for American Muslims at that time, I don't know.

I do know that when she broke the news to me about her family's impending move back to Jordan, she was able to keep her voice even while discussing almost any aspect of it, including the fact that her father would make the choice about whom she married, except for the changes she would have to make in how she dressed. She'd be trading her blue jeans for headscarves, packing away her favorite t-shirts to Goodwill. Living in an adolescent state of narcissistic hyperbole as I did, it had never occurred to me that anyone anywhere lived with more onerous restrictions than the ones I endured. As I looked forward to growing up, I saw my horizons expand. What did Deena see, I wonder?

She told me repeatedly that her mother stood up to her father on one issue. Her mom insisted none of her children be married before the age of twenty-one. Deena seemed to cling to this one fact as if it were her salvation. Her mother would postpone the beginning of her life sentence for as long as possible. Neither of us wanted to get married. The examples we knew were our parents' relationships. But here was a difference. I had a choice;

Deena didn't. Her father would be arranging a marriage for her as soon as she turned twenty-one. I like to think her mom would insist on someone who would treat her daughter well.

I haven't heard from Deena in over two decades, but I often reflect back on my friendship with her.

I wonder how different our lives have been. I'm certain she married at twenty-one. I held out to the ripe old age of twenty-two.

The community I live in now has a diverse population. My home is located only about a mile from the local Mosque. The other day I was on my job at the local public library when I saw a group of Muslim women come in, wearing their head coverings. They all headed straight for the Romance section. I thought then about Deena, and a question occurred to me. If I learned about romance novels from her, how did she learn about them?

ಐ ಚ

Honorable Mentions: Nonfiction

Barri L. Bumgarner

Memoir in Montage

We sat on the edge of the entrance, our four-year-old legs dangling. The flimsy wooden door to the cavernous space below the house hung too loose, like a tooth ready for the pillow. We had pushed it aside, peered underneath, not at all dispelled by the rank smell. Now perched on the ledge like two old geezers on a dock, we cast our Tyco fishing rods, the plastic bobber landing with a plop in the murky waters stagnate under the house. Conversation was unwarranted, so we waited, just like we'd seen our dads do. We sipped sodas, belching like it had the oomph of our fathers' beers of choice.

Neither of us saw our moms, cameras in hand, giggles suppressed. We had fish to catch, even if it looked like nothing was biting. We could sit for hours, sun beating on our faces, imagining the bobber plunging under. We even practiced cussing like we'd heard our dads do. If they could do it, we could do it better.

Oblivious that nothing swam under the surface of the slimy brown water, Christine and I cast and recast. We'd mastered it. Even if we never caught anything, it didn't matter. Our dads never did either.

***

Pyromania ran in our blood. By third grade, Christine had morphed into Wilson, and I . . . well, I had the imagination to take our ploys to the sun and back. My brother had dubbed her Wilson for some inane reason, claiming her signature retaliation *You got to choose a weapon* sounded like *Chastaina Wilson.*

Who the heck is that? we'd ask, but he just laughed. And forever after, Christine was Wilson. Whatever our names, we ate mischief for breakfast. Spring brought the fever that sent us playing outside for hours, undeterred by the cold, unimpressed that our brothers sprinted through backyards in their daily football game. Often we served as the football, but today, we had an idea . . .

Yeah, if we spin it real fast right when we light it, it'll be totally cool . . . We had the matches, the vision, and for unknown reasons to us, the motivation to try this experiment. Pulling a few squares of toilet paper out from the roll attached to the wall, we struck our first match. Before we could get the nerve, the flame fizzled and left a sulfuric trail that tingled my nose.

Try again, Wilson prompted, so I did, snapping the match from between the cover and the strip, a decisive *phhht* preceding a new dancing flame. Without risking wimping out— and never living it down—I reached out and touched the tiny fire to the edge of the toilet paper Wilson held. The explosion of flame, no matter how fast we spun the roll, raged out of control before we could react. In milliseconds, we couldn't spin the burning roll, and in horror, we watched the flames spark higher until they ignited Mom's brand new plastic curtains. Now in full panic, we yanked the curtains to the floor, stomping and screaming. I grabbed a towel, shoved it into the sink, and doused it with water. We draped it over the smoldering pile of curling plastic, the memory etched as clearly on my brain as it was on the carpet.

When the putrid smell of sulfur and burnt plastic became too much for us, we slinked out of the bathroom, too stunned to talk, too terrified to think ahead an hour until my mom got home. Never one to bail, Wilson sat on the couch with me and waited. The instant Mom came in the door, she smelled our crime. We said nothing while Mom surveyed the house, her nose so far out of joint she could smell our trail a mile away. She emerged from the bathroom, the hall, and stood staring at us, her face as red as the flames had been.

"Christine Lisa Larimore, go home. You, young lady, you get back to your bedroom."

Nothing else. For once, Mom was too mad to even talk. Dad would be home in a couple of hours, and if I could play him right, I might be able to survive this mess. Even when he entered my bedroom shortly after eight, his belt in hand, I saw the twinkle in his eye.

I breathed a sigh of relief.

I got a lecture, even got the dreaded "d" word. And Daddy's disappointment hurt almost as bad as the bite of his belt. Not that I would know, but legend had it from the stories Mark and Rusty told. I was twenty-eight before I confessed to Mom that Daddy never whipped me—not that day, not ever.

Being Daddy's little girl helped. And I never lit anything on fire after that.

***

So as the baby in the family, I fell low on the totem pole with two older brothers who majored in rough-housing and minored in taunting. As a result, I had what they affectionately referred to as a 'morning voice.' In my defense, it was a cry for help. I'd squeal as shrill as I could, "Mark, stop it!" or "I'm tellin'!"

Rivaling fingernails on chalkboards, the screech became the stuff of family legend. Even more than that, our imaginations and tendencies to exaggerate made us unique and offered a perspective on our many Bumgarnerisms.

Too often, when Wilson hadn't gotten up yet or had to go home early, I was left to my own devices playing in my bedroom. While my Barbies and GI Joes were fun, my Matchbox cars rivaled the best collection in town, and no one could argue that I had the coolest stereo of any kid my age, I had ways of getting back at Mark for his relentless taunts. Four years older and twice as arrogant, Mark thrived on teasing me. His cruelties differed based on the season—tackling me during football, launching things at me in baseball season, and a variety of pick and rolls, offensive charges, and free throws during the winter. So my typical *Stop it!* echoed throughout our house day in and day out.

Knowing how irritable Mom was after a long day at work, I had the perfect retaliation for Mark. Dad chuckled that we liked to 'get Mom's goat.' But in my game, it got more than Mom's. I could scream for Mark to *Stop it!* And Mom would bark angrily, "*Leave your little sister alone . . . now!*" Mark would be ticked but his teasing abbreviated.

One Saturday morning, I remember clearly Mark chanting his cruel songs, trying to make me mad or cry. Why a twelve-year-old boy reveled in picking on his eight-year-old kid sister was beyond me. The Beatles provided our score, but I was in no mood. "Mark, stop it!" I wailed, hitting a pitch that grated on even my nerves. "I'm tellin', stop it!" I sustained the piercing cries for several minutes until I looked up and saw Mom and Mark standing in my doorway laughing.

Busted.

"What? I was just playin'," I countered, but they continued to laugh. It would take weeks, maybe months, to be able to try this again. But Bumgarners were all about stamina and perseverance. I might be the youngest, but I still had the heredity.

 ⇣ ⇡

Lori Galaske

The Flying Truck

Today is November 27, 1990. The Christmas season is in full swing, although it's not exactly "merry and bright" today. It's actually pretty gloomy, raining off and on. I've already done a little of my holiday shopping. My goal was to be done by Thanksgiving, so I could enjoy the festivities of the season without dampening my holiday spirit by commingling with the battalion of shoppers at the mall. I have the same goal every year. Maybe one of these years, I'll reach it.

It's Tuesday, my day to have the boys. Unfortunately, the weather isn't cooperating with my plan for them to play outside this morning, and being in an enclosed area for any amount of time with two four-year-old boys who firmly believe they're ninjas (one of them a clinically hyperactive ninja) is always an interesting experience, but it pales in comparison to what is about to happen.

"Boys! Quiet down! I'm on the phone!" I yell for the umpteenth time this morning.

In response, I hear an ear-splitting, "Hi-yaaaahhh!" and then what passes for silence in my son and nephew's four-year-old minds. I smile and turn my attention back to the caller.

"So you were saying . . . you're heading out around 6:00? Don't leave before I come by. It should be well before then though. Okay?" It is Bev's thirtieth birthday, and I've just put a cake in the oven for her. I'm off the phone now, and I begin to prepare lunch for my little ninjas. Today I spend hours slaving over the microwave, heating up some Campbell's Chicken Noodle soup and slathering a few saltines with peanut butter.

"Nathan! Philip!" I call them to the kitchen, settle them on their stools at the counter, and serve them their feast. The rain picks up. I walk over to the glass doors that open onto the deck.

The rain is flying by *horizontally*. I touch the glass of the door and feel it shaking. For a moment, I consider taking the boys to the basement, but *no*, I think, *the tornado siren hasn't gone off. I'm sure we're fine.* I'm more confident in the weather service than I am in my own sense of danger. Just then, Marc tears through the living room.

"I left the truck out. The windows are down!" He yells.

I follow him to the kitchen door that leads to the garage. I stand on the threshold, ready to close the garage door for him as soon as the truck clears the opening. Then it happens—in a flash and yet, at the same time, in slow motion. A square of sheet rock drops at my feet. It's the cover to our attic access. *That's weird.* I think. I look up to see why it fell, but my eyes don't get that far. Across the garage, opposite from where I stand, I see daylight coming through the joint where wall and ceiling meet, or perhaps I should say "met". Then I hear it. The roar is deafening. In less than a blink, the garage and all that was in it save our little Toyota Corolla wagon, is gone. Seemingly evaporated. Marc is in the truck, and the truck is sliding toward what used to be the back of the garage but now is a drop off to our yard below.

"MARC! MARC!" I yell—as if he could hear me, as if he's flying off by his own will and I can change his mind about this trip if only he would listen. I envision his body a tangled mess wrapped around a tree somewhere, and I know I will never see my husband again. I turn to the boys who have been knocked off their stools by the force of the tornado blowing through our house. In my best calm, have-it-altogether, don't-frighten-the-children voice, I begin to scream hysterically. When the boys begin to scream too, it comes to me, *I'm the adult here! Get a grip!* With great effort, I stop screaming and close the kitchen door behind me. Although the suction created by the tornado is strong, somehow I'm able to pull open the door to the basement. Then I wedge myself between the door and the door jamb to keep it from slamming shut. The boys run under my arm and down the stairs. They don't have to be told what to do.

Miraculously, Marc is at the bottom of the stairs shouting at us to get down there. We do. The four of us huddle together, shaking, underneath the main beam in the center of our unfinished basement. Water begins to drip from the light bulb above us. Marc runs to the fuse box and turns off our electricity.

Then it's over. Just like that. It's eerily quiet. No one speaks. No one moves. Our eyes wander to the window. We look outside and see the truck sitting on its four wheels looking back at us in surprise. It had never flown before. It didn't know it could, but then, neither did we. We see the freezer that had been in the garage lying on its side. Its contents are strewn, not only over our yard, but over all of our neighbors' yards as well. The turkey I had purchased on sale the week before Thanksgiving to enjoy on some winter day in the near future now lies abandoned. Our home is torn to shreds. We know this because we see pieces of it coating the ground like newly fallen snow— our roof, our garage, drywall, insulation, our *stuff* is everywhere.

Incredibly, the phone rings. It's Bev again. "You're not going to believe what I just saw!" she says.

Somehow I think I will.

శ   ఇ

C. B. O'Brien

The Ring

The ring sits in a prominent place on the shelf of the bookcase in my study. It's a large ring, a man's ring, made of silver (or something that looks like silver). The ring traveled for thirty-five years and twelve-thousand miles to get to my shelf. The journey starts.

Some day in summer 1967 in Chu Lai, Republic of Vietnam:
I am a medic with D Company, 1st Med. Battalion, 1st Marine Division. This is a hot place, a wet, sticky place, a place that has the feel of regret. A place where every day is cherished in its passing—one less day. I am in the triage, the place where we decide who's going to die today and who's going to die sometime later. I'm inspecting the wounds of casualty # *whatever.* The specific nature of his wounds I can't remember—nor is this important. That they are not head wounds will become apparent. Six months in this place have taught me that this guy is in real trouble.

He's a large man, a young man (weren't we all young men?). He's a South Korean, we called them *Rocks* (ROKs-Republic of Korea). And anyone who's done a tour in the Nam will tell you that as warriors, the *Rocks* had no equals. My experience told me this warrior had probably fought his last battle. As if anticipating this, he looked up at me, took off his ring, put it in my hand and closed my fingers around it. He said a few words in what I took to be Korean. Whether it was a request, a thank you or just goodbye, from his words and tone I could not tell. Their worth I inferred from the fact they were his last. He simply did these things, and died. After a careful check of vitals, toe tag and the mandatory towel to protect us from the face of death, I then moved on. I dropped the ring in a pocket and gave it no more thought that day. After all, casualty

 # whatever was only one of probably fifty seen that morning. I only kept the ring that morning because it seemed to be the thing he wanted.

These days I look at the ring on my shelf and wonder that such a sad comment on our nature should be that we can fashion nightmares that boil a man's life down to a few last words falling mutely on a strange face in a strange land. That I was the face in that man's nightmare makes me wonder if I've spent my thirty-five years so well that I deserved them more than *# whatever*. The ring stays on my shelf, not because I will ever guess what those last words were, but because I won't. And I am keeping the only promise that I can; I won't forget.

ℰ ℭ

Other Contributions

Jan L. Coffman

The Old Drawer Key

ଓ   ଔ

Evelyn Aholt

For a Moment

This get-a-way place
embraces a little creek
blooming violets
a watchful deer
Warmth of summer midday sun
refreshing gentle breeze
grass of green beneath bare feet.

I study neglected grapevines on hillside
grape jelly, boot-legged wine
people respectful of earth's supply
I explore the abandoned house
once owned by an African American lady
I hold her rusted muffin pan
rest on the crooked wooden floor
I sit cross-legged near cave opening
thoughtful of the mound of dirt
perhaps burial place of a Native American
scout for arrow heads
I hear my German grandmother
soothing her baby with a lullaby
I ponder an African American mother
soothing her baby with a lullaby
I ponder a Native American mother
soothing her baby with a lullaby
their voices in unison with the breeze
their faith, love and dreams lift high.

For a moment a youthful girl
shares a oneness.

Larry W. Allen

For Mary

And the memory I have
of a willowy blond
standing between two
goateed guitar players,
belting out a song,
her lovely long hair
tossing in all directions.

Tall and strong,
defiant and unafraid,
she sings with such urgency
and conviction.
Like an angry flower
deprived of vital nutrients,
bending to one microphone
then the other,
right fist clinched
and held close.
On a silken rampage
tossing that hair . . .
making Pete Seeger proud.
It's the hammer of justice,
it's the bell of freedom . . .
and she really believes it,
and makes us believe it too.

D.C. Tail

Late on a chilly April night
three street ladies stand in a row.
And one of them says "Honey,
Why do you have your hand in your pocket?
Are you a cop?"
"No," I says.
Only the subway has closed
and I must walk nine blocks
back to the hotel
in the murder capital of the world.

No one is around
and a killer looking dude
steps out of the shadows
half a block away.
He comes toward me
large and sinister.
I don't even have to think about it.
I stick my right hand in my jacket pocket
and Mr. Killer Dude
crosses to the other side.

Forget what your mother tells you.
Always be nice to the street ladies,
and they will be nice to you.

಄   ಚ

Edgar Bailey

October in Chains

The street is wide with large elm and maple trees lining the parkways, leaves changing from green to yellow, orange and red drying to brown and curling off the branches onto the street and yards. The parkway littered with the maple trees' airplane seeds as they helicopter down and rest on the walks, trees shedding their leaves through the fall and during the weeks of November, when the rain has stopped and the leaves have dried in the yards and on streets, we gather them together and create small sacrificial fires to the dark beasties that were released and allowed to roam the earth just a few short weeks before. The leaves must dry for the rain always falls on the last day of October. We pile the leaves in the gutter, where the curb is higher, and light the small fire, supervising it, or so the adults say, but the children know that the ritual demands obedience and observation. Observation not to monitor the fire but to pay homage, an honorific, to the things set out upon the earth. Such is the way children think.

They don't think in those words, but the meaning is clear; to protect our vision of the world we must observe these rituals. For children learn in context, not by definition but through usage, and anything lost in nuance is gained in belief. It is like the child who, peering into the shiny curved fenders of a Packard, realizes the world that we see is so brightly lighted to emphasize straight lines and right angles so we'll not be allowed to see the actual dark, reversed, curved world that it really is. Such are the thoughts of children.

It was another of those dark nights when Papa said to entertain Gramma in her room. Saying in her room was superfluous because every night after dinner she would retire, avoiding the radio, television and modern life, in favor of letter writing and reading. More and more Papa wanted us, Anna, my older sister by two years, and me, to talk to Gramma. So this too became a ritual, obligatory like church every Sunday and every holiday, to endure. Anna offered to tell her about her day, school, school work, her friends and the fun things that happened on the school bus. Gramma would hear none of it and likewise when pressed to tell us of her childhood would instead tell us a tale. One of her favorites was the "Little Boy and the Wolf." It wasn't the boy who cried wolf but an entirely different story she said was told to her in the original Romisch.

"The boy was curious, like a cat and as thoughtless with heavy curiosity, and did not believe that some places hold the scent of evil and death but the light and sweetness of flowers. But we have all smelled the rich, too rich, growth of flowers growing too closely together and too wild, un-pruned that died and dropped providing the only nourishment for the wild growth.

"He was told by the village elders that no good comes from visiting an out-of-the-way shunned place, and there was truly nothing to see. He ignored his elders, ignored at his own peril, set off one morning when he should have been working the fields with his father but instead shirked his duty, his duty to family and to the village and to all the people who depend upon the summer hay for the winter's livestock. But, no. He took off across fields, through the thickets to the place a village stood years before and had been abandoned—abandoned so they said, only because the soil was depleted and thin.

"The sun was setting by the time he'd gotten there and finished exploring the remains of the buildings; even the church roof had caved in.

"When he turned his eyes toward home and his ears toward the darkening forest with its deep shadows, he saw the three men drop to all fours. Their backs arch like cats but grow thick with bristles of coarse fur, grey and white, feral eyes shining even in the gloom. Their teeth became fangs and their mouths snouts. He tried to will his legs to run but to no avail. Panic for his life stayed his feet; he stood there for the rest of his life as the three rushed him. No one from his village ventured there to retrieve his remains."

Anna sat there quietly and then asked if the moral of the story was that he should have been working in his own village for his father.

"No," Gramma reassured her, "that would mean people would never try to do new things or explore what they could actually accomplish."

Then, Anna asked if it were to listen to the people who know more?

"No," again Gramma said, "because your elders are often afraid of anything new and they fear change and even worse, they are often wrong. There is no moral, Anna. It is only a story. It is like life. But, remember, the boy never came back to tell the story."

Gramma liberally dosed her fairy tales with foreign words and phrases. Some words were guttural and harsh then suddenly bitten off so that the words were not so much ended as truncated. One of my sister's friends asked why grandmother barked her English at us. That girl was no longer welcome in our house.

Papa would only chuckle when we asked about Gramma and he would tell us that when she was a little girl, smaller even than Eva, my baby sister, she spoke Romisch and now few people do. Very few people do. And Gramma spoke Lithuanian and Yiddish and ordered store clerks around in their own native tongues.

Her fairy tales, though, were all dark occurring in dark places with bad men or beasts and sometimes in one body both the bad man and the beast and they chased small children. "Not to steal them like they say the gypsies do, which they don't, no matter what they say, because Romany have more of their own than they can feed so why would they want to feed a stranger's child?"

We, her listeners, had no answer to that but she never seemed to need an answer. She went on about the children running though woods and brambles, thickets slowing them and thorns tearing their clothes and flesh.

But the running "was to no avail," according to Gramma. That was one of her stock phrases, a chorus repeated and she would not refrain from her refrain. When the bad man or the wolf in men's clothing or the witch pursued, the child's flight "was to no avail." Likewise hiding in the thorny thicket provided no relief and the sorcerer would part the thorns as easily as Moses would the sea. Not eating the evil broth from the witch's cauldron, after weeks and weeks of self deprivation, with hunger itself finally gnawing the child's stomach, was to no avail. "Yes, yes, my children, they ate whatever foul concoction had been bubbling in the oversize pot in the oversize fireplace. Their attempt to escape was to no avail. It was only after they ate and grew strong enough to push her into her own fireplace could they survive."

These tales laced with indecipherable words were made more ominous because of the possibility for misunderstanding. Any story of chases and flogging and death and destruction still makes me fear. It does not matter whether the words sound like *schmear* and *schlemiel* or *in Spiritus Sancti*. They are foreign words and they make the tale dark.

Max and I ran down Tenebrous Avenue, slipped through the loose boards of the fence into the wooded area behind the church. That copse, now filled with leafless trees but thick brush, separates the church from the convent. We lighted two of the cigarettes cadged from the rectory and stood shivering from the cold and the exertion.

At the edge of the thicket is a stump the nuns used for beheading rabbits; the rabbits they told us were destined for the stew pot. "Even we must ask sacrifices from these little creatures for us to survive," said one of the younger nuns.

Max and I stood with our backs to the church and to the wind, standing with one eye to watch the convent and one to watch the back of the rectory. The fire engine sirens, bells and thick smoke rising from the rectory and most probably a mad scramble to locate the Father before smoke claimed him.

Max and I finished the pack of cigarettes, cupping the matches from the wind while watching the arc of water pouring on the rectory roof. We were careful to put out the matches and the butts because the last thing we wanted was a grass fire behind the church.

I could not see the body from behind the church, but I imagined one black carbonized arm pointing skyward either beseeching or accusing.

November should never come; it releases the demons upon the world. Halloween is a play, a pageant to placate them, to make them think better of us, and to let us reassure ourselves it is only a game. We dress up like them in costumes to gather on their behalf like the old ladies who supposedly leave milk out for their cats but who really are pouring libations to ensure their gardens grow unmolested. Who knows what could sprout in the sour soil left by the others? Who knows what grew in thin, depleted ground?

Even today, years later, in the wee hours when the temperature changes cause floors to creak as though someone is walking nearby, and the wind brushes branches against my window, even today, I think the way a child thinks; I think the world would be better if we could perpetually keep October in chains.

৪০   ୪

Al Beck

Spring Haiku

The sweet smell of spring
with growing-green whispers' thing
tells what June will bring.

* * * *

Who are You to share
my early Spring's festive whirls
with curious squirrels?

* * * *

Soft breeze in the trees
this May morning permits me
to do as I please.

* * * *

Crabapples in bloom
but shagbark's barely budding -
fresh Spring behavior.

₭ ₳

J. M. Brandt

Optimism Doesn't Equal Failure

My laughter plummets onto
their petals, like adorning medals.
Rivers of sunlight twist around, begging

me to lie still
and let the deluge come. But I spin like
a lover, I dance like a child, and I become

air. I choose not
to fade into shyness, or pass my voice
through a whisper's lips.

Flowers that remain
nameless swell onto my lap, curling
over my fingers—I will not be afraid of their

bees and insects.
I will let them bloom on my skin.
I will learn how to trust.

Red Sand

Discovered, uncovered
from the red sand that
curled in my lungs.
Each swallow is a
vivid cacophone,
sliding roughly against my
ears.

Is this my
body?
Is this my
wind?
Am I allowed to feel this
gracious?

Every breath is a question to
be wondered.
Every movement is a hesitant
stretch to ponder
if I *really* am moving.

Touch
me,
let me know the touch of fingers
on my face, in my hair.

Are there still
wings on my back?

    (Were there ever...?)

Sword Swallower

The jealousy slips
in, over
my tongue.
I taste its chill;
the metallic flavor, rigid
and tapping at the back of
my teeth, a Morse conversation
with my struggling esophagus.

It continues, sliding against my heart,
against my stomach, against my longs.
The trick is to breathe it in, suck it down.

I wrap my lips into a ragged kiss around
the hilt, tightly puckered,
but without much respect. There's
a moment I forget
to blink. And I figure either way

I'm dead.

༄   ༃

Carol Gorski Buckels

Christmas, Two Years Later

When my mother died
I thought there would be
nothing left to resist
and pull against
but I was wrong
because she was the
woven chord that kept
us all together.

Now the end
has come unbraided
and we stand with
the yarn in our hands
trying to determine
which end goes over and
which goes under or first.

We are clumsy at it.
We drop the ends
and pick them
up again.
The braid
is lumpy
and misshapen
as it never
was when my
mother was alive,

but we still hold the ends
and keep trying
to get it right
to feel like a
whole family
when one whole
piece is missing.

When Answers Come

We are always waiting
for the answers
but not the ones
that come.

ॐ   ☙

Carol Buening

Life Cycles

Late October dry winds
whistle through demented leaves
      crinkle and sigh

Lament the lost heights of summer
when they stretched and flourished
as fresh green pennants blown taut
fervent in truth and joy hot in the sun

Summer willows bend and flex
straighten into militant rows
march in feathered cadence
Wings tip like geese in autumn

Night Wrap

I startle awake
White sheets gleam under the eye of moon
Wrap the night in wispy tissue

I watch deep shadows sliver the moon
Savor silence for a distant day
Stars burst like phantom lights search a gravel road

I stretch yawn and sleep
Never seeing never hearing two stags
Crash together on the silver ridge

Wilderness Woman

The odor of damp fur in dreams,
renewal of warmth,
comfort soft as Grandma's old wool quilt.
Her own deep breaths, other warm breaths
rustled soft as Spring over her stiff limbs.
Light seeped in through the stone crevice.
Eyes still closed, she wished it away.
Shifted and felt warmth all along her body.
A clutched fist or paw rested against her back.
She must leave. The soft length of it flung
over her as though it would keep her.
Her breathing strained. She swallowed
and eased herself free, not daring to look.
Forced herself to move gently, slowly
along the rock wall. Felt with her shaking fingers.
Moved into light and heard its heavy movement.
Slid herself out. Could it climb? How large was it?
No time left. She ran along the rock ledge seeking a
small crevice or high limbs. Behind her louder strides,
a rock shot from the ledge and fell into the valley below.
She sank down to push herself into a small, dark opening.
Scraped and struggled to force her way deeper.
Held deathly still pressed against cold rough stone.
It lumbered past her. She waited, listened, took deep breaths
and heard it return. It shuffled, sniffed and settled.
She imagined a large furred beast black as a bear.
Sharp white teeth and a ravenous appetite.
Why didn't it dig her out or leave?

The White Elephants

White elephants are not unusual in our home. You might find this hard to believe, but they travel as a herd. This herd has grown excessively.

"Are they alive?" you might ask.

No, not physically alive, alive as memories of the past. Each has an individual history. They do encroach on our living space.

When I look at the oak, Spanish Mission buffet in our kitchen, I remember finding it many years ago at the Boone County Fairgrounds Building where I attended Friday night auctions. At first glance, this buffet was not a pretty sight, but the carving on the front intrigued me. It might go cheap. Yes, I bought it. This is my problem. I buy too many white elephants because they are so cheap.

My husband Jerry was not thrilled. He hauled the heavy, long buffet home and rebuilt the inside to safely contain dishes. I tried to refinish it and wilted in the summer heat in our garage. Once we put it up for sale at our garage sale, but I didn't want it to sell. It did NOT. Later, Jerry did a grand refinishing for the buffet, an antique oak table from his family and oak chairs from another auction I'd attended.

About those oak chairs, they were the last item sold at an auction. Unfortunately, I was supposed to attend a barbecue with my husband. Since I had already spent hours in the heat to buy those four chairs, I would not leave until they sold.

"You guessed it. Right? They sold cheap. Cheap. Cheap."

I loaded them and rushed home to shower and dress. I felt starved. We arrived late. Happily, they still had tasty food to eat.

I love the way silver items reflect the light. I'm not fond of polishing. I have discovered silver plated trays, casseroles, an antique tea and coffee set, pitchers, vases, silverware, small elephants and necklaces.

Like many other women, I like pretty china and glass and have collected. At least, they never need refinished or polished.

The other day, I heard Miriam talking about a cabinet shelf loaded with dishes. She said, "It fell down; I had it fixed; it fell down again." That made me feel apprehensive because our shelves are heavily laden.

I do prefer to be on good terms with Jerry. Through the years, he has sanded, stained, nailed, glued, refinished, hung chandeliers, rewired lamps, wired art work for hanging, and loaded or unloaded numerous strange objects.

I have stubbornly stood outside at auctions in downpours of rain, frigid temperatures so cold my hand shook even holding a hot cup of coffee, and I risked heat stroke or eye damage in searing sunlight at 95 degrees with a heat index of 110.

Oh, as a white elephant collector, I cannot quit, but I downsized and changed tactics. I now prefer garage sales, bazaars and resale stores. I try to limit my enthusiasm to small objects.

Happily, eclectic decorating continues to be in style.

We carried donation bags to St. Francis House, Salvation Army and the Senior Center. Jerry and I are protected from additional work projects by the herd of white elephants inhabiting our house. We still seem a little crowded.

By the way, if you happen to own a large, round brass tray in good condition, I have a beautifully carved table base.

Our memories become treasures held in our minds and our hearts.

౮౦ ౦౩

Barri L. Bumgarner

Premature Calls

I flipped the lights off, anxious to get to bed. My stats test tomorrow warranted a good night's sleep, and midnight served as my cut-off.

Late night rituals: locking the back door, making sure the garage door was closed, turning on the front porch light, grabbing treats for Kaycey and Lilah. Once in the bedroom, I shut the door, switched on the TV, and handed milkbones to each of the "kids."

Snuggling in for the night, I channel surfed, settling for a *Law & Order* re-run I'd only seen once. By the time I drifted to sleep, Jack McCoy had the case locked.

Warbled colors surrounded me as I drove through the fog. Headlights danced in the rearview, the twilight playing tricks on my eyes, cars hovering too close behind me . . .

The sharp ring yanked me from that nether place in dreams. I jerked awake, not sure what it was. I listened, then the faint ringing of the phone near my head, almost muted for just such reasons, sent my heart into my throat.

Shit . . . No good ever came from a phone call in the middle of the night. The digital clock, blurry, read 3:13. I fumbled to answer it, feeling for the Talk button.

"Hello?" My voice, full of sleep, sounded foreign.

"Barri Lyn?" My oldest brother's frantic whisper wedged the panic deeper into my throat. "They got to Mom . . . I called 911, but they're not gonna get here in time . . . "

"What? But they're coming? Who's there? What happened? Why are you at Mom's?" Words tumbled, too panicked to wait their turn.

"I—I can't talk too loud . . . they'll hear me." He mumbled something else, maybe to another person?

"Is Carrie there with you?"

"Yeah, we ate dinner with Mom and had some wine, so we stayed over . . . we heard a window break, voices . . . Oh, shit . . . they're coming . . . Carrie . . " His voice dropped too low to discern.

I strained, desperate to make sense of what Rusty was saying, what it meant, why he'd call me two hours away.

"Hey!"

I jerked the phone from my ear, startled by Rusty's full-voiced shout.

"What the hell're you doin'? Why're you doin' this to us? Please . . ." A grunt followed the high-pitched plea, then the phone went dead.

I sat in bed with the phone still to my ear, the dial tone mocking me. For twenty or thirty precious seconds, I couldn't think. I scrambled out of bed, turned on the light, and punched 911. Too flustered to think, I recounted the last two minutes as best I could. The operator told me to hang up and try my mom's house. She would contact the Lebanon police to confirm they were on the way.

When I dialed the old familiar number, I was stunned to hear Mom answer, her voice groggy, annoyed.

"Mom? Is Rusty over there?" I tried to stifle the confusion in my voice.

"No . . . what's wrong? Is there something wrong?"

"No, but he called, said he was there, said someone was in the house, that he'd called 911 . . ." I shared the rest, until Mom finally calmed me and said she'd explain to the police that Rusty must've been partying somewhere and was confused, or just messing with me.

"Well, tell him he scared the crap out of me!" My heart had finally slowed enough for me to breathe normally. "That's weird though . . . I mean, he's never done anything like that before. He really needs to get a life."

"I know. God love him. I'll chastise him all you want tonight. He and Carrie are coming over for dinner."

An eerie foreboding slithered up my back, but I let it go.

It returned less than twenty-four hours later, at 3:13 A.M., when the phone rang.

හ ෆ

Jan L. Coffman

Alarm Clock

   ⁖   ⁗

Jimmy Capps

Grandpa's Dog

I walk this road every day. Exercise, I need it: diabetes, high blood pressure, too much fat. All that, and it gets me away from an endless list of "need to do" stuff.

It doesn't seem that long ago, that I jogged this same road. That was before the heart attack, when I actually could jog. Back then, I could jog, go to work, do the "need to do" stuff, and still play softball on Tuesday nights. Man, you sure get old fast. Anyway, I was jogging the day I found it.

Someone had dumped it along the road. So, like a dumbbell, I picked it up. I thought I would feed it, get it healthy, and then take it to the Wal-Mart parking lot. There I could find some animal-loving sap to take it, because I sure didn't need a dog.

My wife had a fit when I brought home "that stupid dog," but luckily my granddaughter, the light of my life, was there when I brought it in.

Jennifer was five at the time, and took an instant liking to the pup. She played with it and gave it a name. She called it "Pepper." So there I was, stuck with a dog.

I took Pepper to the vet for shots and all that stuff to make him a regular, owned dog. But I didn't like it. All the time, I kept beating myself up for not having the guts to just walk on by, let nature take its course, but I just couldn't do it. I couldn't leave the little critter to get eaten by varmints right alongside the road I jogged every day. I mean, what would I think, every time I jogged past? I would have a guilty conscience.

I'm just saying, I didn't want the dog in the first place, but then an amazing thing happened. After a couple of months, it grew on me. No longer my granddaughter's plaything or a charity-case, Pepper became *my* dog.

Pepper grew up to be a border collie and a damn good-looking border collie too. He was the best dog a man could ask for, loyal, friendly, and good to kids. Pepper was to me, what my own grandfather's dog was to him. Those two, Grandpa and his dog, were two of God's creatures that walked this very same road that Pepper and I walked, be it many years ago.

This road, the one my grandfather and I walked with our dogs, is connected to a farm that has been in my family for years. When Grandpa came home from the Marines at the end of the big war in 1919, he bought this place for next to nothing. Since then, it has passed from him, to Dad, to me. This farm used to be big until Grandpa sold about half, Dad sold most of the rest, then after the parts that I've sold, there's not much left.

They're all gone now. Dad got killed in a car wreck while I was gone to Vietnam. He was fifty-four, pretty young I guess. Maybe Dad was lucky, dying quick. Grandpa was not so lucky. First, he had to bury his son, and then a few years later Grandpa died too. He was old when he went, and he died slow. They say the old go quick, but that's a load of crap, Grandpa took a long time going, but then, he was one tough old bird.

Just last month when I walked down this road, you know for my fatness, I heard a sound like something was following me. I looked around, suspicious, some would say. I guess I am paranoid, and for sure, I was half expecting to find a FBI man trailing me, but there was nothing there.

The next day, damned if I didn't hear it again. Like something running down the road. Like a dog running. Somewhat slowly, because that's the way my mind works, I started remembering Grandpa and his dog, fifty years gone.

I was in college at the time. During the summers and on weekends when I came home, I hung out with Gramps. He was still young then, in his seventies. They were all alive then, all living here where I live now—Mom, Dad, Grandma, and Gramps. Mom doing her social stuff, Dad trying to work himself to death, Grandma going senile and Gramps, well Gramps, he was my pal.

Gramps was one hellava companion for a college kid. People said he was crazy, not to his face though. He would have kicked their butts, seventy years old or not. Truth is, I guess he was crazy, he claimed to have a ghost dog.

"He was the best damn dog I ever had," Grandpa claimed.

He called the dog Fritz, in honor of some poor German bastard he had killed at the battle of Belleau Wood.

The dog died of old age when Grandpa was sixty-six years old. I was a teenager at the time, and of course, I knew everything. That was before I grew old and stupid, and despite my intelligence, I was amazed at the way the old man grieved.

A few years later, on my trips back from college, I walked down the road to the mailbox with Grandpa. He talked about his dog.

"Come on, Fritz," Grandpa would say to his dead dog. Fritz would walk along with us. At least in Grandpa's mind, Fritz was walking along with us.

"Ain't he the damnest dog ever?" Grandpa would say. "Ain't every dog that would stay with you, even after he died."

I played along, although somewhat sarcastically.

"You got that right Gramps," I said. "In fact, I ain't never heard anyone else ever claim the same for their dog."

"That's cause, dammit, their dog ain't Fritz."

"I wish I could see him," I would say, and look this way and that. "Just where is he, anyway?"

"Hell, I cain't see the damn dog, he's friggin' dead. You cain't see a dead dog, what's wrong with you, boy? You feel him, you sense him. You just know he's there."

"Well he sure is a corker of a dog," I would say, as we walked along in silence.

Grandpa pulled out a chaw of tobacco and offered me a chew. I took it every time, although I usually puked.

I remember one day as I walked with Gramps and his invisible dog, the wind blew softly through the dead leaves that littered the road. I swore I heard something walking beside us.

Grandpa laughed and spit tobacco.

"You hearing things there, boy?"

"Just the wind," I said.

Now, I am the Gramps and every day I walk this same road. It beats sitting home enduring my wife's menacing glare. Today, my fourteen-year-old granddaughter, Jennifer, walks with me, which is a change, since all week she has been hanging out with Rodney, that little earring-wearing juvenile delinquent who lives up the road. This morning, thank God, his mother hauled him off to stay with his dad in Jeff City.

So, as we walk, we hear the wind rustle the leaves behind us. I turn my head slightly to hear better.

Jennifer gazes my way.

"What are you listening for, Grandpa?" she asks.

"Ain't listenin' for nothin' girl. Done heerd 'em," I say. I put on my best hillbilly accent, not real, but an amusing irritant to my granddaughter.

"That there is my dog," I say. "That there'd be old Pepper."

Jennifer shakes her head in dismay, and disgust. She was there that day two years ago when a gravel truck squished old Pepper. She and Rodney, who was a pretty good kid back then, helped me bury him in the back yard.

She has also heard me tell stories about my grandfather's dead Fritz of long ago and knew where this conversation was leading.

"For God's sake, don't tell Rodney about your dead dog," Jennifer said.

"Rodney, Rodney who?" I ask.

My granddaughter renews shaking her head.

We walk along in silence. Suddenly the wind rustles the leaves, and Jennifer turns quickly to look behind.

I laugh and spit tobacco.

"Want a chaw?" I ask my granddaughter, offering her some Beech Nut.

"No!" she says, as she gives me a devastatingly evil look, one no doubt inherited from her grandmother.

The Elevator

The crazy white-haired old man said his name was Peterson. By the time he introduced himself, he had rambled on so, that no one paid attention. Still he talked.

"You can spend your whole life," he said, "and when you look back, most days ain't worth nothin'."

"The important ones," he droned on, "can be narrowed down to a few."

He was old, even older than me. Whereas I was a grandpa, he was a great-grandpa, or maybe even a double-great. The other difference, of course, was that he had gone crazy. I wasn't quite there.

He said he used to be a Judge, or was it a juggler? Maybe I should have paid more attention.

I listened when he said he knew how to open the door, but wouldn't. He said he would when he damn well pleased. Finally, I concluded, he didn't know any more than the rest of us.

How long had we been stuck in this box? I couldn't tell; my Timex wasn't working. It was just looking at me blinking 12:00, off and on, off and on.

I hated big buildings, and this thing was a monster, bigger than anything in Springfield, and here we were, stuck somewhere near the middle. So, there we sat, backs to the wall, the emergency lighting casting a dismal gloom. Every few minutes someone would try a cell phone.

"Metal shell of the elevator," I said, "blocks the signal." Still they tried.

Except for the old man's incessant babbling, there was no sound in the elevator. Out of boredom, I began to study my fellow prisoners.

There were four men, a woman, and a child. The woman and child appeared to be a mother and daughter. The rest were strangers.

The kid next to me could have been a college student; he was the right age. He wore a West Coast Chopper t-shirt, the kind with a swastika. His distinguishing characteristic was a silver stud stuck through his right eyebrow.

I decided to talk; we might be there a long time.

"Do you ride a bike?" I asked.

"What?" Eyebrow answered with a note of incredulity, as if I had asked an obscene question.

"Your t-shirt, West Coast Choppers, I thought you might ride a motorcycle."

"Oh," Eyebrow said, "not hardly."

He was holding his cell phone in his hand. He flipped it open.

"Friggin' Sprint," he said.

Eyebrow just sat there looking at his cell phone as if it were an unfaithful girlfriend.

The question I wanted to ask was—what kind of moron would stick a metal rod through his eyebrow?

That was his business, and it's not like I hadn't done stupid things in my youth, so I explained my motorcycle question. "I ride a motorcycle, that's why I asked. My name is Jake," I said. "Jake Cobb."

"Friggin' Sprint." Eyebrow repeated, without acknowledging my introduction. He stood and moved to the farthest corner of the elevator. He held his phone high in the air and tried again. He flipped it shut and found a new position between the little girl and the soldier. He slid down and settled onto the floor.

Was I like that when I was young? I wondered.

To occupy my mind, I started labeling my fellow prisoners.

"Eyebrow" was the punk-rocker college dropout.

"Great-Grandpa" was the old white-haired man.

The soldier, of course, was "The Soldier."

Sitting across from me was a guy whose shoes cost more that my entire wardrobe, maybe more than my car. A few years ago, I would have labeled him a "Yuppie." I don't think they use that term anymore, and I never liked it anyway, not since it was thrown at me, so I went for his watch.

It was a Rolex, though you can't be sure. Years ago, in Singapore, I bought one for ten bucks. The good ones cost thirty, so you really couldn't tell, his might have been authentic, or a just a good knock-off. Still, "Mr. Rolex" it was.

Completely by surprise Rolex asked me a question.

"Do you go to Sturgis?" he asked.

"No," I said, I fibbed a bit. I had been to Sturgis—once.

"It's quite the show," he said. "My fiancée and I take our Harleys. I have a Sportster for her and a Road King for me. We go to Sturgis every August."

"Do you ride to Sturgis or trailer?" I asked.

"I've got a fourteen foot enclosed Featherlite."

Just as I figured, one of those guys who spends a load on an overpriced status symbol, then hauls it to his destination. Probably rides around town, wearing those sissy leather chaps, posing as some hardcore biker.

Of course, he would look down his nose at me, even though I have ridden across the country twelve times.

That's what I thought, but then, who was I to judge.

"I ride a Honda," I announced, and that, of course ended that. Telling a Harley guy you ride a Honda is like telling an old NASCAR fan that you like Kyle Busch.

The truth is, I did own a Harley years ago, one of those AMF pieces of junk.

I slid into the corner recently vacated by Eyebrow and slipped into a nap. It seems like I was out for a long time, and then I awoke with a thump as the elevator started moving and the bright lights came alive.

I looked around the elevator.

"Where is the old man?" I asked aloud, to no one in particular, which was good, because no one answered. I stood and turned a circle, looking around the elevator, just to make sure, even though it would be impossible to hide.

"Where is the old man?" I demanded.

"What old man?" Eyebrow asked.

Darn, I just noticed, there was someone else missing too. Maybe, while I was napping, the elevator had stopped and let some people off.

"Where's The Soldier?" I asked.

"Weren't you a soldier?" Eyebrow said sarcastically, "I heard you babbling on like you were some kind of hero."

"Yeah, I was a soldier. We all were, but can't recall any heroes. Did this thing stop already?"

I turned to Rolex. Rolex was standing by the elevator door, as if he were the operator. He looked older.

"Where is the old man?" I asked Rolex, only Rolex wasn't wearing a Rolex. His wrist sported a simple Timex.

"Ask her," he said, indicating the woman, who was now holding a baby.

Jesus, I said to myself. Where did that baby come from? Am I losing my friggin' mind? And where is the little girl?

"What has happened?" I asked aloud.

"It is," Rolex stated emphatically, "what it is."

"Why did you leave me?" the woman wailed at me accusingly. "Why did you go to San Francisco to live with those hippies?"

"What are you talking about?" I demanded, as the stud through my eyebrow burned furiously.

"The stud is only a metaphor," Rolex whispered in my ear.

"You should hold the baby," the woman cried, thrusting the baby in my direction.

I recoiled, backing away from the woman and baby.

"Sorry, too late," I heard the old man say.

"You're back," I said as I turned to find the old man, but all I saw was an old man looking back at me in the polished brass of the control panel.

The elevator stopped.

"This is it," I said, or was it the old man who spoke?

"It's time we got off," I heard someone else say.

"Wait," I pleaded, "is there something I need to know?"

"Better figure it out quick, Jacob." That time it was the old man. It was Mr. Peterson again. He stood in front of me.

"Because this is your stop. In fact," he continued, "this stop is for all of us."

My mind raced, strange things were afoot.

"Except for the woman and baby," he explained, "because, they don't exist. Not anymore, except for maybe in the nineteen sixty-eight in your head."

I spun around to look for the woman and baby.

"Gone," he said, "back to sixty-eight, I suppose. Now, Jake, did you figure out that thing you needed to know?"

"The hell with it," I said. "I just want out of here."

I walked to the door, ready to see what was on the other side.

"Oh yeah," I said. "There is one thing. Which way has this elevator been going? Up or Down?"

"Well," Peterson said, with a note of finality in his voice, "for you Jake, we went down. All the way to the bottom."

"You mean . . . " I started to ask.

"No," Peterson laughed, "just messing with you. I took you to the top."

                                                                   ଅ   ୪

James H. Coffman

Movie Star

Over coffee, we men talk
of her skin, her eyes,
the way she walked,

and how she helped us all
grow up back then.

Ninety-seven? Haven't heard
of her in years. Didn't she
go to live with her daughter
in the U.K.?

Emphysema, the paper said;
we thought she'd died.

Household name once,
even rated the *Milestones*
column in *Time* last week.

Happy Days Drugstore

"I'm gonna lift a girlie mag, wanna watch?" Norman whispered.

"Yeah, I'll watch," I said, excited to witness an actual theft at Clark's Drugs. This was the same drugstore where my brother and I, five years earlier, were wrongly accused of taking a comic book. I didn't want to rouse *that* memory. Still I couldn't keep from watching.

Norman was a friend, skinny with horn rim glasses, and spoke with the hint of a plugged nasal passage, not a bad kid, except for his larcenous bent.

The magazines and comics were near the long window fronting on Michigan Street, so I could watch the crime close up from the *outside* of the store. Beautiful setup. Norman eyed the nudie magazines for a while and then chose one to pay for. He ambled back to the magazine rack after paying and pretended to still be browsing. He looked over the top of his glasses to see if I was still there. Satisfied no one suspected Norman folded one of the magazines inside the one he'd paid for. He surveyed the store, stood and slowly walked out the front door. "Piece of cake," he said.

We walked down Michigan Street in the direction of his home. "I've got quite a few of these at home. Wanna see 'em?" I nodded. *Why not?* I was, after all, an adolescent male.

Norman took me to an attic room where he kept a trove of skin mags, hundreds, stacks neatly lined of *Playboys* and *Penthouses* and a lot of copycats. I mumbled something non-committal and left, walking past Clark's on my way home.

It was the 1950s. I like to say I grew up a block from the Happy Days Drugstore. Thing is, it *wasn't* happy at the time. There was just too much uncertainty, too many pimples, too much testosterone and no big brother to tell me what to do with it.

They *were* Happy Days . . . *now*, if that makes sense. It was all about the tube tester by the front door of the store where an adolescent could actually test his old TV tubes and take home a good one and fix the television set. It was about the woman behind the counter who would give a kid a five-cent dip of vanilla and pour a six-cent coke over it for a homemade soda. It was about a friend who clerked at the drug counter and bragged to us about selling condoms to an elder in our church—by the *gross!*

They were happy days even though I never saw Ron Howard or Henry Winkler at Clark's. They were happy for other reasons, mainly the people like Myrt, and Johnny, Jimmy, and yes, Norman too.

ဆ   ල

Cathrine Daily

The Cup

The fading sun fell behind the forest that would take them
into Gannattian territory. Left with poor light, Sir Brandon
Montgomery wasn't eager to enter the unfamiliar and
unfriendly kingdom. Newly knighted and twenty, Brandon
wasn't sure if his first mission was a success. His small party's
flight from Lady Amelia's estate in Caffed to her brother's in
Gannatt had been poorly planned. Dismounting, Brandon tied
the reins to a tree and strode to the edge of the forest. Quietly,
he searched for any signs of movement within. Behind him,
leaves and stones crunched and the scent of lilacs drifted in the
air.

"Brandon?" Lady Amelia's quiet voice broke into his
thoughts.

"What?" he snapped, then sighed. *Manners before anger.*
"What, my lady?"

"Are you all right, Brandon?" She sounded concerned.

"It's inappropriate to use my name so informally." He
continued to search the forest for signs of danger.

"You're quite right. I'm sorry. You've been nothing but kind
to me since my husband's death. Even when I told you who I
was."

"I promised I would protect you and see you safely returned
to your brother." He wanted to take her in his arms
and comfort her, but he couldn't.

"You're still angry with me?"

"Yes. If you had told me sooner, then this might not have
happened. Your stepson wouldn't have started the rumors."

She stepped in front of him forcing him to look at her. "I
wasn't going to tell you, not until Edward made his accusations

about us. He didn't know that we couldn't . . . I had no reason to poison my husband."

"I highly doubt you poisoned Lord Rickard. Not after what you told me." He paused. "The poison was in *my* cup. Someone meant to poison *me*." He ran his hand through his tangled chocolate-brown hair.

"Your cup? The poison was in your cup?" Fear flashed in her blue eyes, so much like his own.

He nodded. "Your husband drank from my cup. Otherwise your secret would have stayed safe."

"Your death would have been worse. Thank the gods you didn't drink from that cup."

He laughed. "It would have been better for me."

"Oh Brandon, you don't understand." Amelia put her hand to her forehead and took a few steps. After a moment, she stopped and looked at him. He feared she would guess how he felt. Instead, she said, "You have to trust me. Bringing more men wouldn't have been safe."

"It isn't safe with me!"

She looked at him again and started pacing. "Brandon, I . . .," she stopped to face him, "need you to be safe."

He had expected something but not that. He didn't want to be safe anymore. "We should be going. We don't know how far Edward's men will follow us."

Brandon led Amelia back to her horse and helped her up. *Don't worry, Amelia, I will find out who poisoned your husband.* He climbed upon his horse and urged it toward the forest. Amelia rode next to him. *She still looks beautiful,* he thought. He shook his head. As if reading his mind, she reached over, patted his hand and smiled. He jerked his hand away. She frowned but let him be.

Darkness fell and a thick fog crept up around them. He turned back to tell Amelia to stay close, but she was no longer behind him.

"Amelia!" he shouted. He brought his horse to a halt and waited, but saw and heard nothing. Brandon dismounted holding the reins tightly. "Amelia?" Still no answer. His sword hissed as he removed it from the sheath.

Something stirred in Brandon's mind. An overwhelming sense of panic filled him. He stumbled and fell to his knees. His breaths came fast; his chest felt heavy and tight. Something brushed past his ear, whispering, but he couldn't make out the words. He turned just as it brushed his other ear. This time he heard the words: *Kill him!* He reached out, but nothing was there. He struggled to regain his composure. Slowly, pieces of memories floated into his mind of a night of death. Like a sword, panic and pain cut through him as the memory pieced itself together. Before he could puzzle it out, leaves stirred and twigs snapped. His horse pulled impatiently on the reins, but Brandon held them tight. Taking a deep breath, Brandon looked up and immediately tried to scramble backwards.

"Easy son, I won't hurt you."

The creature stepped toward Brandon, emitting the sound of twigs rubbing together. Within an arm's length, it stopped. On his knees, he and the creature stood eye-to-eye. Its skin resembled bark. It held a glowing torch in its hand. Brown tights and a green tunic clung to limbs no bigger than sticks. Green leaves dotted its gray hair. A brown hat with a feather sticking from it rested cockeyed on its head. Green eyes stared back.

"What are you?" Brandon leaned heavily on his sword.

"You must be human, creature, are you not, to be askin' such a silly question?"

Brandon nodded and swallowed. *The stress is getting to me. I am not seeing this creature! Talking trees don't exist.*

"Your name?"

"What?"

"Speak up boy, what is your name? Didn't your mother teach you any manners?"

Lately she has taught me a lot. He shook away the bitterness. "Sir Brandon Montgomery, sir."

"Interesting, a Caffedian accent. Wouldn't expect to see you in these parts." It sighed. "Trystan Green is the name. I am a brownie." Trystan held out his hand. "Come now, I only bite when I'm hungry, and it's your luck I'm not hungry."

Brandon hesitated but shook its hand. For a hallucination, the creature was quite solid.

"Very good. Pleased to meet your acquaintance. Now tell me, who is Maggie?"

"Maggie?" Brandon was confused. He didn't remember calling for his mother, but she wasn't his mother anymore. Not since Amelia . . .

The creature snorted. "Not important. What I want to know is if you can do it."

"Do what?"

"Kill someone you care about."

"I wouldn't, not without good cause."

"But you have."

The words *kill him*, echoed in his mind. Brandon shook his head and looked around but still couldn't see very far in either direction. "Where are the others?"

"Others? You mean there are more of you humans?"

"Yes, a female."

"Is she named Maggie by chance?"

"No!" Brandon stood, suddenly tired of this hallucination. The creature stepped back, eyes wide.

"Taller than I thought or do you grow when angry?"

"Taller than you thought." Brandon sighed. "I won't hurt you."

"No? Why can't you admit it to yourself?"

"Admit what?"

"That you kill so easily to get what you desire."

"I can't."

"You don't remember? He didn't fight you."

"I can't kill someone that won't fight me."

"Oh, I think you can."

"I can't do it!"

"You have to remember." The creature grinned. "You killed for something you can't have."

The grin struck a memory. Brandon's head swam as he remembered the serving girl placing the mugs on the table. Amelia, looking lovely in her silver gown, told him it was time to toast Edward and his new bride. He picked up his mug. Edward grinned, watching him. Brandon knew then what Edward had done. Drink the poison during the toast or insult Edward and his new bride? The cup trembled in his hand as he sat it down near Lord Rickard. Brandon slowly picked up another mug and waited. Lord Rickard picked up the mug and raised the drink to his lips. Brandon could have knocked it from his hand but he didn't. He sat frozen, waiting for Lord Rickard to swallow the deadly liquid.

Oh gods! That was before he knew. Before Amelia told him who she was.

Brandon tried to shake away the sleepiness and guilt that overcame him. He blinked, and closed his eyes before opening them again. He grabbed the saddle as he suddenly realized he was still riding next to Amelia.

"Are you all right?" she asked, noticing his sudden movement.

"Aye, I guess I fell asleep. I must have been dreaming."

He closed his eyes, praying for forgiveness. Had he known, he wouldn't have done it.

"Sir Montgomery?" Amelia asked.

He looked over at Amelia. He should have noticed his resemblance to Amelia before she told him she was his mother. "It was just a bad dream." Unlike Amelia, he was going to keep his secret.

It was the only way he could show he loved her.

ဆ ©3

Elizabeth Davis

The One That Got Away

I slammed my front door. Windows rattled. It is a wonder my new double-wide did not implode. Seeing him again hurt. Or maybe it was anger.

I could not get my computer on quickly enough. In the beginning, I had written for therapy. "Write through the pain," I had been advised. "It is cheaper than a shrink."

I started typing.

"I can not believe this. It has been . . . let me think . . . seven years. Why did he come here? He did not even go to college here.

"Back in high school Ron and I had been *the* couple and, before going off to separate colleges, we had discussed our future together and planned to get engaged at Christmas.

"I did not date at college, because it was supposed to be Him. Us. I could not wait for Christmas vacation. Apparently, neither could Ron. He brought his wife home. Not his friend, not his girlfriend, not even his fiancée. His Wife!

"That is the real reason I quit school. I went back, just not as a student. I found a job at a bookstore just across the street from campus. The owner talked me into taking some courses in business management and I threw in a couple on creative writing as well. The rest, as they say, is history.

"I now own not one, but two bookstores. I have published two nonfiction books, a murder mystery, and just signed the contract for its sequel. I am even seeing a very eligible bachelor."

I stopped typing and re-read what I had written. Then I saw it.

I smiled as I settled down in my favorite reading chair with a pot of hot tea by my side.

He is not the one that got away. I am.

಄   ಅ

Linda Fisher

Ladies Night

The redhead pressed her butt onto the edge of the polished oak barstool. She stretched her short legs to the limit and boosted herself onto the wooden throne. Her burgundy dress rode up beyond what would be considered decent in her normal surroundings. The bartender moved toward her, blocking the muted TV causing her to miss the special bulletin scrolling across the screen, "The FBI announced today a person of interest will soon be brought in for questioning in the St. Louis Lady Killer serial murder case. Six women . . ."

The bartender swished a cloth across the surface of the vintage mahogany bar, craning his neck for a better view of his customer. His handlebar moustache bounced in cadence with his raspy voice, "What can I get ya, pretty lady?"

Her eyes raked the shelves of multi-colored bottles filled with spirits. Nodding toward the hand lettered sign, Ladies Night— Two for the Price of One, she said, "I'll have a frozen raspberry Margarita, and you might as well line up the free one. It's been that kinda day."

"I hear ya, lady," said the man on her left. "Name's Barry Newton."

She swiveled her chair counterclockwise to size up this Barry person who had intruded into her private world. Barry smiled showing teeth so white you can almost see the whitening strips. He was so gorgeous she wondered if he could be a model or gigolo.

Deciding the kid looked harmless enough, she said, "Rita."

A jazz band played softly in the background and a few couples danced on the tiny hardwood dance floor.

"Hi there," said an older man settling onto the stool next to Rita. Vick's bottle blue eyes saved him from mediocrity.

Muscular tanned forearms protruded from the rolled up sleeves of his khaki work shirt.

"You must be . . . Stan," she said, reading the name embroidered beneath a Gateway Construction Company logo. The bottom of the shirt strained across Stan's Corona belly.

Completing the introductions, Stan encased Rita's tiny hand in his larger one, which was not nearly as rough as one would expect from a construction worker.

"Well, Rita, what brings you to St. Louis?"

"Am I so obviously a tourist?"

He laughed. "Yes. Besides, you came from the direction of the tower, so I assume you are a hotel guest."

"Observant, aren't you?" She sucked on the straw. "Mmmm, delicious. And two for the price of one for the ladies."

"Well?"

"Well, what?"

"What brings you to St. Louis?"

"Oh, that. A convention." She crossed her legs and the dress rode higher.

"Will you dance with me, Rita?"

"Sorry, no," she said.

"She promised me this dance," Barry said. He leaned around Rita to direct his remark toward the unwelcome intruder.

Barry placed his hand on the small of Rita's back and led her to the dance floor. The warmth of his hand penetrated the thin silk of her dress as he held her close while they dance.

"Mmm," he said. "You smell wonderful."

Rita smiled. "Thanks." Barry might be young, but he was certainly charming.

"My turn," Stan said, intercepting Rita as Barry led her back to her spot at the bar.

"Only if she wants to dance with you," said Barry.

The older man's voice and eyes turned hard. "Aren't you up awfully late for a school night?"

Rita's laugh was brassy as she touched her mouth and the tiny zigzag reminder of a man's jealous anger. Stepping between the two men, she said, "Let's dance, Stan."

Although she wore four-inch spiky sandals, Rita's head barely grazed Stan's chest and his belly bumped her breasts. He leaned toward her and they shuffled around the floor.

"Can you believe that?" Barry asked the bartender.

"No accountin' for taste," the bartender said. The sheen from the silk dress of the elegantly dressed lady contrasted the man's worn shirt and blue jeans.

Barry moved further down the bar and refused to make eye contact with Stan who glared in his direction intermittently. Barry didn't want to fight the big man even if Rita was a sexy lady.

Rita and Stan danced, occasionally sitting out a song, sipping drinks. They engaged in superficial banter but avoided in-depth conversation. Rita never mentioned Stan's wedding band, and he appeared not to notice the rings on her left hand.

Rita yawned. "It's late and I have a session at 8:00 in the morning."

Glancing at his watch, he said, "Wow! Where has the time gone? I hope you don't require much sleep."

"Actually, I'm on a different time zone so it seems earlier to me."

She slid off the barstool, grabbed her handbag, and shook hands with him.

"I need to be going too," Stan said. "I'd feel better if I walked you to your room. Junior over there is still watching you."

"That's . . . thoughtful of you," she said. As Rita and Stan headed toward the door, Barry and the bartender talked intently. Their eyes followed Rita and Stan as the couple crossed the ornately decorated lobby filled with lush tropical foliage. Colorful lights transformed glistening waterfalls into liquid rainbows to soothe travel-weary souls with a bubbling lullaby.

They swooshed to the twentieth floor. The glass elevator provided a panoramic view of twinkling city lights. Plush carpet silenced their footsteps as they walked toward Rita's room.

"Here we are," Rita said quietly. "Thank you again."

"Good night, Rita. Maybe we can get together tomorrow night."

"I'm flying out tomorrow afternoon," she replied, her regret sounded phony. She extended her hand for a final handshake. "Thanks for the wonderful evening, Stan."

Stan used her hand as a lever to pull her toward him. He touched her face and caressed her full red lips with feather light strokes. Dropping his hand, he barely grazed her breast. It might have been an accident, but probably wasn't.

Rita dropped the credit card shaped key. Stan grabbed it from the floor, slid it into the lock and pushed the door open, waltzing her backward. He kicked the door shut.

"What do you think you're doing?" she asked.

Stan grabbed her and began to gnaw on her lip. She slowed the unusual lip action by refocusing his attention with her tongue. Soon the silk dress fell in a crumpled heap on the floor snuggled up to his cotton work shirt.

Early the next morning, she didn't hear the phone ring. Her head rested on the naked shoulder of the man whose strong tanned arm was wrapped around her slender body. His cobalt eyes stared at the ceiling as he listened to a soft rock radio station.

He rubbed her back with large clumsy hands. "Your phone is ringing."

She opened one eye and glanced at the clock. It was her wake-up call. She picked up the phone and slammed it back onto the cradle.

She rolled over in bed, pressed her naked body against his, tenderly rubbing the expanse of his soft belly.

"You're going to be late," he said as he kissed her neck.

"I've been late before," she replied.

The early morning sex combined gentle touches and manic tussling on the bed. They prolonged the intimacy with a shower, using gel for massage oil. Blasts of steamy hot water turned their flesh red, while goosebumps popped up on wet exposed areas.

Smelling of soap, they sprawled on the bed wrapped in towels. Her cell phone interrupted their relaxation. She held the receiver to her ear and said, "Good morning, sweetie. How's mama's favorite guy today?"

Her face glowed as she talked to her six-year-old son. "Want to talk to Daddy? Okay, hold on."

"Hi, son!" he said, caressing Rita's neck while he launched into a discussion about SpongeBob SquarePants. "Yes, Mommy and I are having a great time. See ya this afternoon!"

"Gerry, I've really enjoyed our get-away." She intertwined her fingers with his.

"Me too, Cindy, baby. Although I thought I'd have to thump that kid's head for hitting on my wife."

She laughed at the thought of him being physically violent. He was a gentle giant compared to the ex who had left the scar on her lip.

Pulling her close to him, Gerry sent lightning bolts of pleasure through her with his touch. Absorbed in each other, they did not hear the special bulletin on the radio, "The FBI has arrested Barry Newton as a suspect in the Lady Killer serial murder case."

"Where on earth did you get that shirt?" she asked.

"I paid a man named Stan an obscene amount of cash for it," he said. "Where did you come up with the name Rita?"

"From my drink, of course." He pulled the towel off her and tossed it aside.

"Margarita Rita, I think we have time for one more round before we catch the plane."

∛ ∴

Jan L. Coffman

Pen Points

ॐ ॐ

Grace Fogle

Unicorn Hunting

The unicorn is a mystical creature, one of the few scraps of magic left in this world. Most of humankind are not aware of them or do not believe in them. There are only a few people who do, and most of those people have decided to hunt unicorns. Most scientists will say that unicorns never existed, but people who believe in them know otherwise. Unicorn hunting is a large issue, and unicorns are fast becoming extinct. Humans are getting killed over the items taken from the unicorns, and magic is beginning to leave this world altogether.

The biggest problem with unicorn hunting is that unicorns are almost extinct, and soon there will be none left. They are amazingly rare already, and if they are gone, that means the end of a lot of things. We are not sure how the hunters are finding them, but they do find them, and they then kill the unicorns. Some people do it to prove that they can, some people do it because they do not want to be proven wrong about unicorns' existence, some do it because they want money, and some do it because they are scared. The bottom line is that with all of these people hunting unicorns, there are not many left, and they are getting rarer by the day.

When people hunt and kill unicorns, they normally take several items of value from them. Most often they take the mane, tail, hooves, and horn. Hunters can sell these items for a lot of money. Unfortunately, with how rare these things are, many people want them, and sometimes people are willing to go to extreme measures to get what they want. Such is the case with these items, especially the horns. Their horn is what makes the unicorn magic, and the horns have many magical properties. Many people are willing to kill for these objects, so anyone who is in possession of them is in constant danger of losing his or her life. In fact, people kill for these items quite often, but luckily, unlike some things taken from magical creatures, a unicorn's magic can not be corrupted, can not be twisted, can not become black magic. Because of this, a unicorn's magic can not be used to commit murder, which is quite a relief for the entire world.

An effect of unicorn hunting even worse than people being murdered over the magical items taken from the unicorns is that magic is beginning to leave the world altogether. This can be partly attributed to the fact that many people have stopped believing in magic, and so it does not exist for them, but it is also because of the unicorns dying. Unicorns hold most of the magic of this world within them, and there are already so few that most of the magic is gone. Every time a unicorn dies, it takes another bit of magic with it. The strongest magic unicorns maintain is the magic of love, and when the last unicorn dies, love will completely vanish from the world, along with all forms of magic.

Most believers say that with the unicorn population diminishing quickly, people being killed over magical items taken from unicorns, and the magic in the world running dangerously low, the world we know and love is doomed. People are hunting unicorns left and right and taking magic from the world right under our very noses, and nobody is doing anything about it. Few people are working hard to protect unicorns, and you will know when the last unicorn dies. When it does—which believers are hoping becomes an *if*—life will have no meaning. In fact, life won't even exist anymore.

Unicorns are beautiful, magical, amazing creatures, and those who believe in them do not want them to vanish. As says the slogan of the believers, which is the last hope for life, "save the unicorns." This is not to be confused with the popular slogan "shave the unicorns."

ℬ ℭ

Ida Bettis Fogle

At the Flea Market

The Jolly Green Giant, verdant as ever
keeps company with the Pillsbury Doughboy
still rotund. The time on the tarnished pocket
watches is decades behind the startling glare
of tie-dye Beanie Babies in the next case.
Chenille bedspreads and black ceramic poodles
that used to grace the bedrooms of everyone's
older sister thirty years ago rest near
smoking stands owned by everyone's dad in the
same era. The stoppers in glass jars comma
apothecary elicit a question—
does neither acid comma sulfuric nor
acid comma hydrochloric eat through cork?
A decaying wooden croquet set never
to be used again, or the mallets surely
would splinter, rests beneath a shelf of Barbies,
mint condition, Holiday and Harley, toys
made never to be used at all. JFK
reposes on a salt shaker. In the last booth
you could stock up for the apocalypse with
bedpans, snow shoes and manual typewriters.

ᘯ   ᙣ

Lori Galaske

Spring Break "Vacation"

Marc was hunched over the steering wheel, every muscle in his body tense and wired. I sat beside him just as tense and praying under my breath that God would spare us from glaciation in this vast wilderness commonly known as Tennessee. Ami, nine, and Nathan, six, sat in the back seat in utter silence, which was in and of itself cause for alarm.

Just that afternoon, the atmosphere in the car had been so different. "Looks like we're headed in the right direction!" Marc had chuckled as the snow began to fall. He is an avid fan of heat and sunshine, and the fact that we were headed south, leaving the frigid temperatures and icy precipitation behind us, made him downright gleeful. Planning to drive through the night, we'd left as soon as school was out that afternoon and merged onto I-70 along with other spring break vacationers. By morning, we'd be with my sister and her family in St. Augustine, Florida—sunny and warm and wonderful Florida. At least that was the plan.

The funny thing about life, and particularly family vacations, at least ours: it doesn't always follow the script. Marc and I kept reassuring each other that we were headed south; thus, the snow *had* to stop soon. Yet the further south we got, the more intensely the snow fell. I can't imagine how confused the poor geese must've been!

It was now past midnight. We hadn't seen another vehicle for over an hour, and we were driving in a full-blown blizzard. Snow covered all the highway signs like a warm blanket tucking them in for the night. "There!" I shouted as I pointed at what appeared to be the skinny legs of an exit sign up ahead. "You can just make out a strip of green at the bottom, and there are lights beyond it!" An exit, with lights, meant civilization and hope of survival. The exit ramp itself was indistinguishable,

and we had no idea if it was to the right or the left of the sign.
Marc gambled our lives that it was to the left. We should've
gone to Vegas. He chose wisely.

This glorious ramp led to a hotel, gas station, and restaurant.
We'd hit pay dirt in Chattanooga! Over the next three days, we
became quite adept at such cultured recreational pastimes as
hangman, tic-tac-toe, and trashcan basketball. Of course, *three
days* trapped in a hotel sans pool, game room, or even a lobby
to speak of with a boy recently diagnosed with ADHD is
another story. We each, including Ami, came dangerously close
to a felonious act at some point during our stay. We chose
instead to run races through the halls and stairwells. Our fellow
strandees seemed more than a bit irritated with us, but it was
better than the alternative.

We dined on the sucrose, glucose, fructose, and lactose that
the hotel vending machines offered and on the fine cuisine
served at the one-star restaurant across the parking lot. Their
array of gourmet entrees included: hamburgers a la pork
sausage, grilled chicken breast a la pork sausage, sirloin steak a
la pork sausage, and of course, pork sausage.

On Monday morning, Tennessee reopened their highways.
Once again packing our bags and our car, and picking up our
dormant hopes, we slid our way onto Highway 27. An hour
later, the newscaster on the radio announced that the state had
closed the highways again. The packed snow was now solid ice;
but we soldiered on, weaving in and out, dodging frozen pot
holes. Thirteen hours later, we'd driven 118 miles.

Another six and a half hours, and we'd covered the remaining
380 miles—miles that were gloriously absent of precipitation in
any form. Our bodies were numb, but we'd arrived. Marc laid
on the horn as we pulled into the driveway. My sister and her
family ran out to greet us; we uncurled ourselves from the car
and collapsed in their embraces.

After a dreamless sleep, we awoke the next morning ready for
the beach, the sun, and Florida fun. Donning shorts that exposed
our white, sun-deprived, obviously northern legs, we stepped

outside . . . and immediately back inside, whipping the door shut. It was cold out there! Trying to comfort us, my sister assured us that it had been seventy and sunny just the day before. Yeah right.

Later that afternoon, with the cold of the morning a distant memory, Marc and Nathan decided to go for a swim. I know you're thinking that it must've warmed up quite a bit. Oh no, no, no. They were just determined to swim. We didn't drive through a blizzard to be stuck inside all week. Such was their reasoning. The fact that the thermometer read forty did not deter them at all. So while the rest of us stood around the pool wearing jackets, sipping hot cocoa, and keeping our goose bumps company, Marc and Nathan took a dive and slide, respectively, into my sister's outdoor, unheated pool. A split second later they shot back out as if they'd hit a trampoline. They dashed inside while we, the spectators, meandered back in, our hands curled around our warm mugs.

Another "must do" on our list was, of course, Disney World. We piled into our cars and off to Disney World we went. The good news was that we didn't have to contend with long lines. The bad news was why—it was cold and raining. My sister had purchased our tickets beforehand, and we either went to the park that day or forfeited Disney World altogether. We made the best of it, wearing sweatshirts and rain ponchos as well as tennis shoes and socks that were thoroughly soaked. A little advice—don't do Disney World in the rain. It really loses something.

By Thursday evening, we'd all but given up the vacation we'd imagined; and in a desperate attempt to salvage the week, the four adults decided to go out for a nice dinner. We'd leave the disappointments of the week behind us, enjoy good wine, good food, and good company. We piled into my brother-in-law's car. He started up the engine and backed out of the driveway . . . straight into the side of a car parked across the street—ours.

"Just drive, Mike. Don't stop. Just drive." Marc didn't even look out the back window. Mike hesitated. "GO!" Marc yelled.

Miraculously, dinner went without incident—though we learned that Florida does seafood much better than they do beef—as did the entirety of the following twenty-four hours, most likely because we stayed in the house, under covers, trembling in fear of the unknown evils that lurked outside in this malevolent state.

We packed that evening and said our goodbyes early the next morning. The driver's door barely stayed latched due to the crunch from Thursday evening, but it would make it home. As we headed north, the road that less than a week before had been a sheet of ice, was clear and dry. We planned to drive straight through, stopping only to gas up the car. We wanted nothing more than to get home to the amiable north and back to work so we could relax.

Hour after hour, mile after mile, the drive home was smooth and quiet. It was bliss. Nearing a rest stop just outside Cadiz, Kentucky, we pulled off to use the facilities. As we rolled into a parking spot, a horrific metal-on-metal screech filled the air. I thought, "Oh man! Somebody's got problems. Geez. That sounds awful." The kids and I walked around the back of the car to make our way to the restroom. I stopped short. Marc was on the ground looking underneath the car.

"What are you doing?" I asked.

"Didn't you hear that?"

"That was *us*?!"

Not only had the brakes gone out, but they'd gone out on a Saturday night at 5:00.

A couple of hours and what seemed like hundreds of phone calls later, the four of us crammed into the cab of a tow truck along with the driver and made a ninety mile drive to a mechanic who'd agreed to work on our car the next day.

We made it home eventually, and when we pulled into our driveway, we stumbled out of the car and kissed the ground, chanting, like Dorothy, "There's no place like home."

The Shepherds

"Did I tell you about my little Hezekiah?" I asked. The night was dark and clear. We could see for miles from our post on the hills outside the city.

"What could there possibly be that you haven't told us about your 'little Hezekiah'? You talk about him every night. Even the sheep are tired of hearing about that boy." My friend answered.

"If you had a boy like my Hezekiah, you'd talk about him every night too. You're jealous of me because I have a son, and all you've produced are girls. Who will take care of your flock when you grow too old, eh, Daniel? Who?"

"My girls are fine and strong. They will make excellent shepherdesses. Even so, I'm still young and viral. Miriam is with child again and the Lord may see fit to give me a son this time. Then you will be the jealous one!"

"Why would I be jealous of your son? I have a boy of my own who can do anything he puts his mind to." Daniel and I bantered like this every night. It was the way of our friendship.

"Can you two not have one night—just one night—without arguing about something? I think I will take my sheep to another hill just to be away from the sound of your voices!" Poor Lazarus, he hated listening to our friendly disagreements.

As the night wore on, the temperature began to fall. We moved around, each of us checking on our own sheep. We met again sometime around midnight to enjoy the meals our wives had prepared for us. We ate in silence, enjoying the beauty of the night.

"The sky is glorious tonight, is it not?" I mused.

"I don't remember the last time a night was as clear as this. Can you count the stars, Abraham? There must be thousands and thousands; but look at the one that shines over the city. It carries the light of a thousand tiny stars. Have you ever seen such a thing?" Lazarus asked. We all looked to the star of which he spoke.

Suddenly, a great light pierced the night sky, knocking us to the ground. We lay there, covering our faces, not daring to look. None of us spoke, but I could feel the fear of my friends as palpably as I felt my own. What was happening? Then a powerful voice spoke to us out of the brilliance. "Fear not, for behold, I bring you good news of a great joy that will be for all the people." I chanced a peek and saw, standing before us, a man, yet not a man. Pure white light emanated from his robes. His face was radiant with joy—indescribable joy. The man continued. "For unto you is born this day in the city of David, a Savior, who is Christ the Lord. And this will be a sign for you: you will find a baby wrapped in swaddling clothes and lying in a manger."

"The Savior?" Did he just say, "The Savior?"

As he finished his proclamation, a multitude of heavenly beings appeared and surrounded him in the night sky. We could no longer see the stars or darkness of night for the brightness that radiated from the angels. Then they began to sing. The melody reached deep into my soul. "Glory to God in the highest, and on earth peace among those with whom He is pleased."

Just as quickly as they had appeared, they left. I lifted my head and looked around. The night continued on as before. Nothing had changed. Had I dreamed it? *Could* I dream such a thing? I glanced over at my friends. They both knelt with their faces to the ground. I could see their bodies still trembling.

"Daniel, Lazarus, they're gone," I whispered. They slowly lifted their heads and sat back. None of us had the strength to stand. We didn't want to stand. We wanted to enjoy the peace and joy that the presence of the angels had brought. It lingered, and we basked in it.

Finally I spoke. "Did the angel truly say that the Savior is born?"

"Yes. Yes he did." Daniel answered me. Lazarus nodded his agreement.

"So we were just visited by an angel who spoke to us and told us that *The* Savior was born; and then a host of angels appeared with him, singing of the glory of God? Am I dreaming and you're both in my dream or is this real? Did this really just happen to us—to shepherds?" My heart pounded within me as the meaning of the angel's words began to take hold. Tears began to roll down my cheeks. Daniel and Lazarus both nodded yes to my question. We stared at each other for a moment. I saw a single tear slide down Daniel's cheek.

I burst out in laughter and jumped up, dancing. I couldn't be still with such music in my heart! Daniel and Lazarus joined me. Joy overcame us. We were giddy with it. We sang. We danced. We twirled and ran around. We yelled out, unable to contain the thrill within our souls.

"Wait! What are we doing?" I yelled out as the words of the angel came back to me. We all stopped. "The angel told us that the Savior was born this day in the City of David. It's the star—the star hovers over the crib of the newborn Savior King. What are we doing here?!"

We took off running towards the star, trusting our sheep to Yahweh's hands, certain that He who sent angels to tell us of the birth would watch over our charges while we went to see the long-awaited Messiah.

Although the city was crowded because of the census, it was easy to find the babe. The star guided us straight to Him. He was wrapped in strips of cloth as the angel had said, and he lay in a feeding trough in a stable. We stood in the doorway, staring at the child, scarcely able to take in the magnitude of the scene before us. The sense of peace and joy that had saturated us moments before was even more intense here than it had been out in the field. The baby's mother motioned us in, and we fell to our knees before this tiny child who is our Savior.

৪১ ৪৩

Svetlana Grobman

Diary of a Russian Immigrant

June 20, 1990

Arrived in Columbia, Missouri. A group of people in shorts met me at the local airport—presumably, my sponsors. They don't speak Russian and I don't speak English, so it's hard to know for sure.

July 4, 1990

Apparently, Americans are celebrating their independence. I've never studied American history, therefore I'm not quite sure from whom. American Indians? The temperature is 41 degrees Celsius. They measure everything in Fahrenheit, and my thermometer reads 105—which makes me feel even worse.

August 18, 1990

A small tornado hit the town. Nobody got killed, but several houses lost their roofs. Some people say that we may have an earthquake here soon, too. Reconsidering my coming here. As bad as it was in Russia, we *never* had either one!

September 6, 1990

No Russian-speaking engineers needed. Had two choices: going to work for Merry Maids or a nursing home. Chose the latter. Now, I'm a nurse's aide working the third shift. Which is good—the residents sleep and nobody speaks English.

October 31, 1990

A neighbor with a daughter dressed in a black cloak came to the door looking for candy. They didn't look hungry, so I'm very suspicious. After they left, I looked outside—the street was *full* of children searching for sweets. Apparently, they have shortages in America, too.

November 22, 1990

Got invited to a Thanksgiving dinner. The food was baked turkey and *orange-red* potatoes. Even in Russia, where red was very popular, potatoes were *white*! I skipped the potatoes and ate the turkey that was stuffed with bread. That way, I suppose, they can feed more people.

December 25, 1990

American Christmas comes before New Year's. In Russia, it came after, and nobody celebrated it.

February 1991

Learned some English phrases, quit the nursing home, and got a job at a public library shelving books—that way I do not have to talk to anybody; although one young woman did ask me where the restroom was. It was just around the corner, but I panicked and gestured towards the reference desk.

September 1991

What a language! Half of the words have multiple meanings, while the other half sound the same but mean different things. Besides, no matter how I twist my tongue, I can't roar the American "r," or hiss their "th." My "think" comes out as "sink," and even when I say "Hi," people ask where I'm from.

October 1991

American expressions are weird, too. When did they ever see "raining cats and dogs"? And what about "give a leg up." Why would I lift my leg if somebody needs a ride home? Also, "it costs an arm and a leg." We never paid with our limbs!

Yesterday somebody said, "I dropped the ball." I looked. No ball. What did she drop? Where?

December 1991

Got promoted to the Front Desk. Understand about 25%. Today, a patron asked about groundhogs. I knew "ground" and also "hogs," so I sent him to a grocery store. Expect to be fired every day.

October 1992

Started reading books in English. Also, made my first "Library will close in fifteen minutes" announcement. Everybody left immediately—including some staff. They said that it "sounded scary."

December 1993

Decided to go back to school and get a Library Science degree. Went to the local university and filled out an application. Spelled "Library" just fine but not "Sience." Got a funny look from the admission staff.

December 1994

Took the GRE. Scored 95% on Math and 15% on English—confused "hair" with "hare," "tale" with "tail," "wonder" with "wander," "desert" with "dessert," and "whipping" with "weeping." Passed anyway—they counted the average.

January 1994

Going to school part time, working at the library full-time—now at the reference desk. Yesterday, a nice-looking gray-haired lady asked me about whales. I took her to the animal section. Who knew she was going to Wales? No time to eat. Lost five pounds.

December 1995

Became a naturalized American citizen. At work, a patron asked how to "dress" a deer. I said, "Do you mean clothes or stuffing?" Another patron wanted pictures of a stagecoach. I knew "stage" and "coach" (like coaches in sports), but couldn't imagine them together and had to ask for help. Lost another five pounds.

September 1996

Last semester. Preparing for the Comprehensive Exam and dating an American. Ran out of "I was sick" excuses and told my professor that my paper was late because I was getting married. He understood. Not sure what I'll tell him next time. Maybe, "I'm getting divorced?" Lost five more pounds.

December 1996

Got my Master's degree! Voted for Clinton and he won. Also, received a marriage proposal. Well, I don't know, but it felt good.

Fall 1997

Was promoted to a reference librarian—doubled the salary and the fear of being fired. Married the American, too! Now, I speak English 24/7. Gained five pounds.

Fall 1998

My husband does a great job of correcting my English—especially when we argue. Also, dreamt in English for the first time. Is that what happens when you marry an American citizen? Gained five more pounds.

Fall 1999

A guy wearing a "lion" cloth tried to enter the library today. As soon as I got home, I described the event to my husband. He was very surprised—not with the guy, but with the cloth. Then he said, "Did you mean *loin*?" Gained five more pounds.

Spring 2000

We moved to a house by the edge of the woods. Now, I'm spending all my free time landscaping our yard. Lost five pounds.

Fall 2000

Deer ate everything I planted. We voted for Al Gore, but he lost.

Summer 2001

Found one kind of bush that the deer don't like. Planted them *everywhere.*

Summer 2002

Tried new plants, and so did the deer. The plants are gone; the deer are still around.

Summer 2003

Went bird watching with my husband. Saw three ducks, five geese, and one woodpecker—all of which live in our neighborhood, too. Put up a birdfeeder in the back yard, so we don't have to drive anywhere.

November 2004

No birdfeeder survives. We keep losing them to the deer, raccoons, and squirrels. Voted for John Kerry and he lost, too.

Summer 2005

Deer destroyed everything, again, so no landscaping is needed. Used my free time to write about the deer eating my "lushes" plants and sent it to the local newspaper. The story got published, although they replaced "lushes" with "lush."

Summer 2006

Now, we are having moles and "aunts" problems. Wrote about that, too. My husband read my story and said, "I think you meant 'ants.'"

Summer 2007

Continue writing. This time, I wrote how my husband and I "tied the nut" ten years ago, and how "exiting" that was. Showed it to my husband. After he stopped laughing, he suggested replacing "nut" with "knot" and "exiting" with "exciting."

Summer 2008

Wrote an essay about what life was like in the former Soviet Union, especially for Jews. The essay got published in The *Christian Science Monitor*, and I got my first fan letter. Opened it with shaking hands . . . and read that the only thing missing in my life was converting to Christianity.

Summer 2009

Spend all my free time writing. No time for working in the yard, watching movies, and even weighing myself. Is that what it means to be a writer?

ꙮ   ꙮ

Sharon Kinney Hanson

Ode for Helen Stephens

Draw near, Catullus,
you mortal of immortal words,
you Roman god who died
for love of Lesbia. Live.

Listen, fide lover
of mounds, this river deep
swiftly runs. Lift this Helen of Troy
who died a thousands deaths.

And quick. Untie her
shoes, her winged shoes,
for her need like ours is.

Veritas Odium Parit *
—in memoriam to Princess Diana

In truth it felt most odd to hear you say,
"I never was a Di-watcher, nor I
a Royalist"; to find your words turn cold,
inordinant, surprised that I processed
her princess funeral-train, a virtual
witness, a participant in real time,
a wake, to see unfold this love event
of sound impact, import to all, to great
political Britannia's sphere; and you,
most-dear poet, friend, reduced with words,

claim no royal bent, yet long for Russia
and decade upon decade do decry, O,
the toppled status of your grand pa-pa?
To make a point about pompous class—yours
presumed proper, highborne, divinely cast,
and mine bastard-based, hellishly rung—I slung
a Latin phrase at you, *Ubi convenimus crastina die?*
which stung and so provoked you to refer to me,
as prayed and hoped. I translate here: *Where*

do we meet tomorrow? for you had said, *Who*
knows what millennium brats will memorize!
to make a point. Perhaps it is too late . . .
There is a changing of the guard, though no
mind-change on this thing of differences—
Mexican or Jew, Irish rich or poor protesting
long academic catholic views or
lasting illiterates—unless all bow
to each and see all sad faces, turning.

* Truth begets hatred

Sonnet

I, being born a woman and distressed
by all the needs and notions of my kind,
am urged by your propinquity to find
your person fair, and feel a certain zest
to bear your body's weight upon my breast;
so subtly is the fume of life designed,
to clarify the pulse and cloud the mind,
and leave me once again undone, possessed.

Think not for this, however, the poor treason
of my stout blood against my staggering brain,
I shall remember you with love, or season
my scorn with pity—let me make it plain:
I find this frenzy insufficient reason
for conversation when we meet again.

৪০ ୯୫

Debra Hardin

7th Sense

Can you hear her voice?
she no longer can, but
were you to ask past lovers
they would say she never had.
His voice was of unreasonable
pity, perhaps to trick her
to think she had no voice
worthy to speak. She had
asked many questions to which
answers felt like a hummingbird's
song, a voice to warble and trill.
A wee creature who spends life
at the violent edge of winds
and swayed branch, and so she hummed
a song that sought her own small greatness.
She lives now in deep silence,
her fickle constant companion which
asks after things lovers should know.
She remembers how full of life she
felt when she no longer had to
hear his voice, full of unreason and pity,
she remembers she no longer had to feel
small and inconsequential. A scar is what
remains of the stained canvas whose brush
greedily mixed up sounds in her broken ears.

Do they know that she now lives
in a world of seventh sense, where
no sound penetrates, no voice
resonates, where her sight has become
a motion picture in and of her mind,
screening the abundant life that dwells
within her beauty, her seventh sense came to life.

ೞ   ಛ

Jan L. Coffman

Fountain Pen

     જ    ଓ

C. B. O'Brien

Phu Bai Romance 1967

We got a big kiss from Lyndon Johnson;
the deep, lingering sort that stays with you,
keeps you up rewinding
the dalliance.
That sweet face—right there,
the generous back-home laugh
or wrinkling something too private to put out,
then slam-bam,
that big sloppy kiss
and out comes the whole story—
pumping out its obscene narrative,
those last little clues still gurgling
in your hands,
      in your head.
      Or maybe a gut-shot,
      man, the smell!
      And nothing but pink and shit
      and it's 3 a.m.
      and trying to dream of anything else.

"Fallujah, Iraq (AP)   Three car bomb attacks
near a bus station today in Fallujah killed
at least 43 people and wounded 89, coalition forces…"
Different romance—same wet kiss.

God and Free Will

Consider the God of Abraham. Be He Allah, Yahweh, or Jehovah, He is possessed of certain characteristics according to His devotees. Being the master creator of all that exists, He necessarily possesses omnipotence (logically including omniscience, omnipresence and just about any other omni you can think of). That God is all-powerful is not an issue much debated among the ranks of believers.

Now at the other end of the scale, on the less impressive page of the menu sit we: Homo sapiens, human beings, Man. Not many will argue that Man has anything like omnipotence, however neither is he impotent. Man is considered by western theologians to possess the very important capacity for free will, the capacity for choice. It would be in fact impossible under western theological belief for this not to be the case. Free will is necessary to fulfill the capacity for sin and to demonstrate moral responsibility.

Now here's the rub. These two situations are logically impossible. If I truly have the ability to choose course *A* over course *B* for example, then God has no power or foreknowledge of my choice. Conversely, if He does have that power, then I do not have a free choice for He can direct my action. God can be omnipotent or I can have free will, but not both. These two capacities are in logical conflict and cannot coexist.

Or can they?

Actually, they can. If I am God. This would eliminate the conflict. Logical though it is, this may sound a bit ridiculous, but consider the existential concepts of some eastern religions, particularly Buddhism and Zen. In these belief structures, Man and God are the same. In fact, Man and everything is the same. We are just a part of the whole of existence and any separation of these is merely an illusion we've created in our minds. Much as there can be no print on this page without the white background, Man (and everything else) cannot exist separate from the background of all the rest of existence. Thus, we are all God.

Rejoice!

The End of Mimsy

I saved my last regret for all the souls
who tramp too late among the deeps and greens.
The clan who dwells there with their instinct
and their shrinking history
cannot hear tomorrow
and do not have a name for my deaf ear.
A world is offered—hung and bled;
her carcass is your future—your bequest.
Your future's future has already fed
my leisure and my lust.
Through the last light, will the children's eyes;
lit by the fathers' triumphs and my greed,
blaze with our passion, unapprised
that from that swollen pride, the hot rains bleed?

ᘒ   Cʒ

Debbie Parker

Simple Beauty

Wake up your mind to the unsupervised surrounding beauty.
Take the ordinary
and create the extraordinary
as the ancient Egyptians did with the timeless majestic sphinx.
Combine function
with beauty
to transform earthy green chips of jade
into Aztec mosaic ceremonial masks.
Take pieces of curlicued brass buttons
to style Buddha's hair.
Sculpt his alabaster elongated earlobes
and full sensuous lips.
Mine stone
to create China's infinite underground army
of horses with flaring nostrils
and soldiers to stand sentry
over the emperor's troops.
Chisel solid marble
to craft Venus de Milo
and David
to warm even the coldest heart.
Smelt gold into regal crowns and chalices
set with blood red rubies
and royal blue sapphires
to tell of an existence few knew.
Use innovation
to see beauty in a pearl brooch
or the tattooed chest that holds it.
Exposure to beauty
and nature
will open your eyes to the ordinary.

Pie Safe

The Farmer's Almanac hung from a string attached to the wall next to the seed calendar in the dining room. Both her home and this one had similar dining room tables except this room had something special, a pie safe. When Elizabeth first heard the name for the cupboard, she thought it must be a joke. Her grandfather liked to pull her leg. She decided that something with such a tempting name definitely bore investigation.

Of course, it was a safe so she had to investigate it on the sly. Lizzie sidled up to it and pretended to look out the window. Yes, the green beans were coming along nicely and the tomatoes needed a little more sun if anyone should catch her in her mission while she was sizing up the cupboard out of the corner of her eye.

There had to be a key because it was, after all, a safe guarding a precious pie. Why else would a piece of furniture deserve such a luscious name? Ears alert, she scanned the room. Nobody was in sight so her small fingers eased towards the door. Elizabeth knew from years of stealthy raids on the cookie jar that she needed the right amount of patience and agility to pull off the heist.

Slowly, she eased the door open, surprised that there wasn't a lock. After all, it was a safe. What could be more valuable than ambrosia in a pie shell? Her grandmother was a good cook. No, actually, she was the best one in the world. The safe had to hold some precious offerings—a juicy cherry pie with golden lattice top, blueberries fresh picked from the garden bursting with flavor or coconut cream. No, that would require a freezer. Oh well, the freezer could wait until another day.

Almost there, she could taste the sweet tart cherries already. When Lizzie opened the door wide, all she found was a recipe box and some dishes. "I can't believe it!" she mumbled to herself. "Dinner," her grandmother called.

Oh good. Maybe she'll serve pie.

Labels

Slapping labels on others makes some feel secure.
They paste them on like names tags at a convention.
The labels sting like a wasp.
"I know you.
You
drink *bottled* Chardonnay—gourmet snob
like Italian stilettos—vain fashionista
like skirts—Victorian frump
prefer pants—butch lesbian
are blond—stupid bimbo
listen to NPR—bleu stocking academic
right winger—red necked conservative
left winger—tree hugging vegetarian."
Labels, once firmly placed,
artfully decorate like a tattooed Samurai.
They know you.
Thoughts cross their lips and Blackberries at high-def speed
saving their brains.

Neighbor

Why do you look right through me
not at me?
Sitting in your lawn chair throne
passing time and judgment you
notice when I work in the garden.
Why don't you raise a hand
instead of an eyebrow?
You copy my landscape
plant for plant, except
yours are fuller and brighter.
Where have I gone amiss?
Did I not give your granddaughter
enough Halloween candy?
Or is it another unknown slight?
Let the winter of our lives compete
for life as our crocus do each year
as they break through the frozen earth.
How can nations negotiate if
you can't even raise an arm in greeting?

ℰℬ   ℭℬ

Teresa Shields Parker

Falling

Lying on my bed, tossing and turning, I drift off to a place where dreams will take me from indecision and dread. Now as the dark blueness of the night begins to envelope me, I am lifted, floating on a mound of fleece and satin whiteness surrounded by the smell of Baby Magic and the touch of tiny fingers. Up, I rise above where life resides. The earth fades away. Colors soften, buildings dim, sounds mute and the faces of those I know fade away. Quiet. Rest.

I float through a vast expanse of the heavens. Something awaits me beyond the next galaxy. A place of answers? I want to experience it. I ask, timidly, may I see?

Before me looms a place. It was there before, but I did not see it. Now it exists. Below, the city reaches for miles in all directions. As I get closer, the colors rise so brightly I cannot stand the intensity. I close my eyes but still see their brilliance, the most exquisite I've ever experienced. They fill my every pore and ooze out around me. I cry out, but make no sound. Yet, the colors do seem to dim.

More, I want more. I do not say it aloud. But suddenly all around me is sound. It is sound indescribable in its magnitude and intensity, unlike any I have heard. It is a song and yet not a song, rising and falling, it builds and fades, growing stronger with instruments no man has heard, in melodies unknown but glorious, in harmonies perfectly intertwined, they seem to wind in and out of each other like a garland of ivy. I know each person around me is part of this complete sound that each is somehow contributing to make this song completely beautiful. It is the sound of community and it fills me, resonates through me, spills out from my eyes and my ears and my mouth bringing a sense of connectedness to me. I want to be connected, but if I were I would surely die because my body cannot contain the sound.

I want to fall on my face, but cannot, for I am still floating above the city. I am here and I want to experience all I can, so I ask. I am allowed to come closer to the tops of the building in the city, and I can see they are not made of glass or steel or anything known on earth. I reach out to touch one of the buildings near me, but my hand goes through it. I realize I cannot on my own feel this place, and so once again, tentatively I ask and reach out again. This time, smoothness that is beyond any feeling on earth wafts through me. I want to rub my whole body against it, but instead, I lay my hand flat on the surface and I am engulfed in the feeling. I try to remove it but I cannot. It is as if a magnet has drawn me to its surface and I feel my body slowly being drawn to it. I am afraid that I will meld into the surface become a part of it. I cry out and am jolted back away from the buildings. But now I can see inside.

The surfaces do not contain, as much as gather, people to them. There are no cubicles or offices, but people come together to do corporate tasks, and a oneness seems to have been achieved. In one building, I feel much knowledge is contained. It seems to vibrate with the pulsing vein of humanity. I notice people touching screens that seem to be inherent in others, storing knowledge in each other, building a sense that all are connected, that all know.

From the central building comes a rumbling. It builds like thunder but louder and more enveloping. The brilliance in the city wanes and fades as darkness covers it. All activity ceases in anticipation of something, though I know not what. I watch faces to have a clue to what my reaction should be to what would seem a coming doom. I am frightened beyond belief. As much joy and exhilaration as I've felt since I've been here, I now feel that much dread and fear. It fills me up, and I am overcome with the knowledge of my own mortality.

It is hot, but I don't know why. The temperature since I got here has been perfect in every way. I can smell burning flesh and hear cries of those in torment. It seems so out of place in this city of perfection and beauty. Then, as if a new day were dawning, the thunder ceases. The stench of burning is gone and the perfect day returns.

Then, He steps forward. I know in an instant it is He, all the city combined in one being. All the city falls on its face before Him. He approaches each person, extends His hand and draws them up to full height wrapping his arms around them. I see the nail prints in His hand, the dried blood at His side, the crown on His head, and I know who He is. In this city of incomprehensible wonders resides the Man of incomprehensible sacrifice.

After He wraps them in His presence, He looks each in the eyes and whispers in their ear, "Good job, My child. Good job." Then He simply smiles at them. The looks on their faces tell their story. He is all they could ever need. I am still floating above, but I so want to be there by His side. I want Him to look in my eyes, surround me with His presence, whisper gently to me and smile at me. Oh, how I want His smile. It is a deep longing in my being—that smile. I have gotten everything I asked for. Being so bold as to know He would never deny my request, I ask for this as well.

The moment I ask, I am catapulted out of the city and I fall, not on soft, billowy clouds, but headlong, a speeding bullet through the blackness of night. Stars whiz by, meteors zing off me, sending searing pain through my flesh as I gain more speed through the emptiness of space. I cannot stop. I am being shot through the heavens at a dizzying rate. I should be burning up now, I think, for I am rocketing toward earth at enormous speed. There is no way I can still be alive. Surely I am dying. Surely this is a part of my demise, and I will be where?

Where would I go? It would be nice to be in the place I just visited, one that the God of the Universe has wired to His command, where all is connected to Him and to each other. This would be the place of ultimate purpose and goal as a direct center for command of the universe, powered by His presence, His smile.

It is clear there is a choice here, and it is clear what it should be, but how to choose while falling headlong through the universe is quite a different matter all together. Obviously, I was thrown from His presence headlong into the universe. But it was my choice really. My choice—because I have chosen not to completely choose Him. I am afraid of the other choice, but now I can no longer smell the burning stench nor hear the beautiful melodies and so the choices have become less of a reality. With the sure pull of gravity, earth beckons me forward. I remember the feeling of that place. It's a nice feeling, but to be there means to totally give myself over to Him in every way. Am I ready for that?

If I could just stop for a minute, I might be able to make a choice, but right now all I can think about is dodging the next meteorite, because, man, do they hurt. I want the ringing in my ears from this rapid descent to stop. If I could just stop for a minute, grab hold of a star, or sit for a while beside the lunar sunset; then, I could choose. And surely I would choose the right thing, the Sacrifice, the Man with the Power, the One who will smile at me when I choose. But right now life is going too fast, and I am falling.

ଚଠ ଓଃ

Von Pittman

A Hazard to Navigation

Phillip Roth's *The Great American Novel* chronicles the misfortunes of the Port Rupert Mundys, who became a baseball team without a home when their unprincipled owner leased their stadium to the government during World War II, forcing the team to play all of its games on the road. An actual professional baseball team suddenly lost its home park in the summer of 1993, a year when the Mississippi truly was mighty. Like many other people, the Quad Cities River Bandits, of the Class A Midwest League, suddenly found their workplace flooded and unusable. Aerial photographs of the sunken John O'Donnell Stadium numbered among the most dramatic images of that terrible summer.

I've watched baseball, at many levels of amateur and professional competition, in dozens of ballparks in the United States and Canada, but John O'Donnell is my favorite. In its 1931 opening, a crowd of nearly three thousand watched the Davenport Blue Sox outscore the visiting Dubuque Tigers, 7-1. Despite several renovations over the years, John O'Donnell— now, sadly, officially renamed Modern Woodmen Park—retains the look of a 1930s ballpark, with a covered, curved grandstand and bleachers down both foul lines.

I prefer sitting on the first base side of the grandstand. From there, as Yogi Berra is alleged to have said, "You can observe a lot by watching." You can look out over the third base bleachers and see engines shifting boxcars on sidings, or watch traffic crossing the Mississippi to and from Rock Island via the Centennial Bridge. Best of all are the tugs pushing improbably long rigs of cargo barges. From the same seats, downtown Davenport, perched on the side of a steep hill rising from the waterfront, looks like a miniature San Francisco in a 1940s *film noir*. With all of that—and a cold beer—you almost don't need baseball. Even if the game is dull, your time—especially on a Sunday afternoon—is well spent.

Baseball at John O'Donnell came to a sudden halt in 1993. That June, it rained almost every day in eastern Iowa, western Illinois, and points north. The muddier-than-usual, suddenly swift, Mississippi flooded the railroad yard, the parking lot, and then the outfield, the diamond, and the lower rows of seats. The ballpark was surrounded by the Mississippi. It became what the Coast Guard calls a "hazard to navigation." The river rose quickly, but took more than a month to recede. There was no more baseball in John O'Donnell that year.

In baseball, however, as in all forms of professional entertainment, the show must go on. The symmetry of the game demands it. Baseball's wonderful—and frequently obscure— statistics demand it. The same number of teams must begin and end a season. Even more importantly, professional baseball is a business. The Houston Astros, the major league affiliate of the River Bandits, could not simply call off work. Minor league clubs are called "farm teams" for good reason. The major league clubs use systems of four or five minor league franchises of varying size and quality to cultivate talent. The minor leagues—or "bush leagues"—are where the majors separate the wheat from the chaff, the sheep from the goats, the pitchers from the throwers. The Astros could not simply abandon players, managers, coaches, and various other contracted employees, and upset the personnel development and evaluation of their entire multi-team farm system. The River Bandits had to play somewhere.

The 1993 team was not burning up the league when the flood hit. Like most minor leagues, the Midwest League divides its season into "halves," with the winners of the two halves playing a championship series. In the first half that year, most of the games were played before the flood. At the end of the first half, the Quad Cities River Bandits stood fifth of seven teams in the league's Southern Division, with a winning percentage of .385.

In the second half, after the flood, they played a few home games at one of the local high schools. A picture shows fans sitting in folding lawn chairs behind the backstop, much like Little League parents. However, like Roth's hapless Port Rupert Mundys, the River Bandits played most of their games on the road, in the parks of their competitors. The loss of their home field didn't hurt the quality of their play. In the second half, they improved to fourth in the Southern Division, with a percentage of .477.

The season closed in August, when the South Bend White Sox won the Midwest League Championship. The River Bandits' players—like their counterparts on the other 13 teams— scattered. Some expected to be called to the Astros spring training camp in February; others hoped to be; and, some knew their days in organized baseball had just ended.

The fans in Davenport, Bettendorf, Rock Island, Moline, and East Moline (oddly, the Quad Cities consists of five municipalities) knew that while their favorite players would probably not be back, their ballpark would be. In 1994, John O'Donnell Stadium would be reclaimed from the muck, spruced up, and ready for play. The boxcars, tugs and barges, and twinkling headlights on the Centennial Bridge would be back. The river that had made baseball impossible to play the preceding summer would again make their park one of the greatest places in the world to watch the game of baseball. The team would play at home again.

Temp Work

The tall man with the neat white mustache retained his regal, but casual, bearing as he walked out of the Blue Anchor at eleven in the morning. His easy, elegant manner had struck me when he went into the cheap waterfront bar less than five minutes after it opened at eight a.m. While his face and eyes now showed slight signs of heavy drinking, his carriage and movements did not. Some people have a presence that causes others to see authority, competence, and integrity, whether that individual in fact possesses those qualities or not. I needed such a man.

He walked the thirty feet or so to a bus stop bench, pivoted smartly, and took a seat. He crossed his legs, reached for his sock, and extracted a pack of Pall Malls and a matchbook. I took a seat at the other end of the bench. "Hello, sir. You look like a seafaring man."

"Screw you, Sherlock Holmes," he said. "Everybody in San Diego knows sailors keep their cigarettes in their socks. And don't call me 'sir.' I'm an Electrician's Mate First Class, not a damn officer."

"I'm sorry I offended you. I've spent considerable time at sea myself. I kept my cigarettes in my sock until I quit smoking."

"Scared of cancer?"

"The wife," I said.

He snorted.

We sat without speaking for at least a minute. Then I said, "You've let me know you don't like small talk. So, could you use some work?"

"I got work, buddy. I'm on the *Abraham Lincoln*; we shove off for the Persian Gulf Thursday."

"Just for this evening," I said. "Five hundred dollars for two hours' work, if we do it right."

He tapped the ash on his Pall Mall. "I'll listen."

"I'm going to tell you precisely what you need to know to get the job done," I said. "And that amounts to very little."

My company depends upon discretion. No, make that "extreme secrecy." If you have ever heard of paramilitary security companies like Blackwater, we are something like them. But unlike Blackwater, our name has never been seen or heard in the news media. Our operations—and even our existence— remain on deepest background.

We supply operatives, or "contractors," to businesses and governments with sophisticated security needs. This can go up to—and include—the disappearance of troublesome individuals. Our contractors include former SEALS, Delta Force operators, and CIA agents, as well as veterans of the British Special Air Service and a few other elite commando units. They are skilled mercenaries who keep their work to themselves.

Given our demand for secrecy and professional expertise, why then was I trying to hire a graceful drunk with excellent bearing who would soon be steaming overseas for months? And why pay him so much? While our regular operatives are always professionals, sometimes we can use an amateur—or "temp"— whose skills match a specific task. When we hire temps, we pay them well, tell them almost nothing, then part company, quickly and permanently.

We met at 1600, as specified. The navy electrician had cleaned up well indeed. He was sober and neat, in a rented pinstriped suit, as instructed. His bearing was elegant and his movements polished. "Your name is George Hollister," I said. We went over his script at a table outside a Starbuck's. He mastered it quickly, with minimal assistance and repetition. We drove my rental car to Chula Vista, which *Forbes Magazine* had once named one of the country's most boring cities.

George was the picture of relaxation on the drive. "Why do you hire strangers for this job? Any flunkey could do it."

"It just seems to work out better," I said. He let it drop. When I found the house I was looking for, a woman in her late fifties answered the door.

"Ma'am, my name is John Harmon; I represent CAE, Consolidated Alberta Energy. Mr. George Hollister is with

Dominion Insurers, also headquartered in Alberta." Both were shell companies with elaborate websites. "Are you Beatrice Adams?" I knew she was, of course.

She invited us in. "Are you here about Phillip?" She told us she had received a telegram from CAE, notifying her of her son's accidental death at an oil drilling installation in Indonesia. "I've been expecting you."

I recited my company's cover story. She cried, obviously not for the first time. When she asked for more details, I relied on the cover story, improvising as needed. We could not tell her, of course, that her son had been killed in a firefight with anti-government guerillas in Central America.

When she ran out of questions and came to a pause, it was time for my new contractor to get to work. "Mr. Hollister" opened the expensive leather briefcase I had provided him and took out two documents.

"Because oil field work is inherently dangerous, CAE takes out substantial policies on all its employees through Dominion Insurers," he said. "Phillip listed you as his sole beneficiary. I have a check for you, made out for $750,000."

The amount stunned her. It almost always does in these cases. This makes the next step almost automatic. Sam unfolded the second document. "If you will just sign this disclaimer, forfeiting any future claims of liability of any corporations or governments associated with the project Phillip was working on, and disclaiming becoming a party to any future investigations, I can turn over this check and we can leave you in peace."

My temporary contractor's manner and bearing were those of a practiced professional, credible and reassuring. He placed the disclaimer on the coffee table in front of Ms. Adams and presented her with an expensive fountain pen, already uncapped. She thanked him, and then signed on the line he indicated. Like the others whose signatures I've needed, she did not notice that Dominion Insurers was not named on the disclaimer. Instead, it bore my company's real name, thus making it imperative that grieving relatives sign without reading it. This document is now secured in our files in the event we ever should be threatened with a government investigation.

When we got back to San Diego, I drove "Hollister" to the old Fleet Landing. I handed him an envelope containing ten one-hundred dollar bills. He counted the contents and thanked me for the bonus. I made him sign a cash receipt and a pledge that he would never discuss this job.

"I know you are curious, but the extra five hundred should help with that," I said. "You are a smart guy; you can tell we are a serious company."

"Damn straight, Sherlock," he said. He folded the bills and placed them in his right sock. "Secret agent for a day."

He made a quick, graceful departure.

ଔ ଔ

Eva Ridenour

Blooming

"I'm wearing deodorant today," she says
as she jumps from the back seat and runs
around the car. Tiny cherry shaped
earrings that match the pink of her Easter
dress bounce on ears pierced as a Christmas
present. Thin, all arms and legs, she reminds
me of myself when I was that age. On her
feet, she wears flip-flops that are popular
even when its cold enough for closed toed
shoes. She'd worn cloppy black heels to
church earlier but admitted on the way out
they made her feet hurt. When she spends
a night with me, she still sleeps with the doll
I bought when she was a baby, but more and
more often I see less and less of the little girl.

ஐ ௧

William Edward Samuels

A Blonde Artist Who Died Young

I love the weaver in her grave,
The love whose life I could not save,
Who threw her pearls before the swine
And now who never can be mine.
When the countess in her blue jeans
Was waiting for a train
My heart and mind collided
And I went half insane.
Eternity has met her,
And she has left her dorm,
No fox will fear her hounds now.
No painter mocks her form.
While I'm the one who's cursed to live
And somehow must learn to forgive.

Veronica Strega

Nearest Approach

I now open
the door to step
into the wild
home, dusty trace

of footprints dried
on the porch, kids'
tracings, a game
of dinosaurs.

Now I open
the wild home
in my heart, the
river of mud, soul

and substrate feeds
my place of chime,
lotus, drum,
and well, my road.

Lovers On The Grass

In Peace Park, he searches
for silver earrings, discarded
gold rings, dollars
lost, the result
of a slip up, a hole
in an untouched pocket
barely bound
together by thread,
untied on the uneven pavement.

Ears covered to the receding
murmur of traffic, to the bright
chatter of sparrows,
he listens for the click
of buried treasure.

He cannot hear
the lovers on the grass,
the soft sighs
when arms wind,
and the thrum
satisfied lust.

Blue Corn Girl's Lullaby

Shadows stretch in the sunlight
like lazy cats, catching
amber leaves that frolic
in the deepest, darkest corners.
She yawns, longing
for her bed of earth
and the dream drift
of snow through winter
midnight moonlight.
Hearing our song, she smiles,
secure in her secret joy, that we
will see in the shining motes
of the season's circle
settling on spider's fairy webs:
this darkness is the seed
of tomorrow's green spark
and another living flame of gold.

Hecate's Moon

The mother of pearl
and tides gazes
with a radiant eye
at the bitterness
you've sown, surges
waters with revenge's
tune, twisting the notes
of your *Clair de Lune*

on the rack of truth.

Your herbs bloom their shadowy lies, reveal
plunder you'd possess. Another woman's husband,
another woman's child.
Your seduction,
a sour tonic,
healing disguised.
The pang is bitter: your lungs
fill with illusion's narcotic
smoke. Your desultory
swipes at midnight
aimed,
like a drunk's
to a lost key.
You'll be empty-
handed, and the moon,
a vessel of vengeance.

Before Me

Inside, I find,
hidden or forgotten,
dusky and still
sweet, a broken stick
of incense, to mark
the place. Stopped for:
    boredom
    interruption
    sleep
    an animal's wail
    a child's sob
or to preserve
the glittering drop
of connection like
a pearl in a shell?

Inside, I find
a reminder from winter,
marking the forgotten
place, the notation
and reminder
for another life, for unknown
stories, the mirror travelling
into reflection's depths
of other, alive
in a tangle
of words like a flash
of mermaid's
scales, a song in vibrating
silence, the ripples
before me.

₲   ₳

Swiftwalker

Morning Touch

As the light glows in the softness of dawn,
as the lip of the sun kisses the horizon,
and the earth shimmers with pleasure,
so do I snuggle in the soft of your skin
and revel in ecstasy from the light of your touch
learning each day that love at our age
can be so lovely and lush.

ॐ ☙

Cathy Thogmorton

Rest Home

They are the already-dead
Surrounded by cheerful
Competent countenances
They await their fate
Miss Mary with legs like string
Flails her way down the hall
An unruly flamingo
In a fluffy pink robe
Mr. Bob sits e-motionless in his chair
Rolled from spot to spot
As though he cared where
Mind gone on ahead
Mr. Peter pees in his pants again
Smell of urine
Smell of death

They are the already-dead
Sitting in chairs
Lying in beds
A whir of machines
Humming tunelessly
Keep bodies alive
Watching cartoons on TV
Fingers fidgeting
Fate assured
Watching what others cannot see
Floating past their eyes
They reach out to touch images
Not yet real

They are the already-dead
Nervous friends
Assaulted by sounds and smells
Unfamiliar
Unbecoming
Pat their heads and speak
In forgotten language
And you, sweet father,
Wait with blind eyes
And icy smile
To re-greet your other half
We sit
Bleary-eyed, tear-tired
And stare out the window
Waiting helplessly for death
To make his nightly rounds
To pass over again
Or make a permanent stop

People move in
Bodies move out
Too late
Too late
We realize
We, too, are the already-dead

Anam Cara

Friend to friend
(soul to soul)
This gift I give you
A box
Not expensive, not lovely
Simple wood
Smelling of pine trees
And soft earth
And-promises

Friend to friend
(soul to soul)
Sandpapered unevenly
By the (loving) hands of time
Dented in one corner
From an earlier fall from grace
Scratched, scarred
A nick along the edge
Worthless
Priceless

Friend to friend
(soul to soul)
This gift I give you
Guard it well
Unlatch the tiny rusted hinge
And you will find
Nestled within, wrapped in
Delicate dreams and pink tissue paper
My heart

౭౦   ౦౩

Jan L. Coffman

Writing That Letter

ℬ   ℭ

Martin Turner

Causation

On all the world's
   hurt and need
Observe the stamp of
   pride and greed
And shudder at the
   void within
Where lurks contempt
   for fellow men

Lar Glendal Wallace

Welfare Queen

Sweet ruby lips and rotten desires
spoiled by the pleasures of life and men
she sits,
dressed in goodwill glamour
laced in store-bought ho pumps
on a headragged throne, hoping
good times and cheap wine will make
an empty evening roll by
spewing "whatevers" and "hell with it"
idle words and clauses, spoken while
laughter and frivolous notions disguise
themselves on a decorated face

The queen takes her stroll
A wood planked balcony, eyeing
cigarette butts and beer cans all smashed
with Welfare's nastiness and pain
she trades a one-night stand
for a nine month burden,
born while scrapping the bottom
of life's barrel for the many
looks of love and guile
settling for top of the line
poverty and systemized shame.

I have traveled to harlem

I have traveled to harlem
on the back of langston's poetry
carried with promise from the voice
of a dream deferred,
my heart is enriched with pride
by a soulful heritage
dared to dream despite,
the vicious attack on a people's
quest for a new beginning
reborn anew—that great
harlem renaissance yes,
I climbed high on the nailed
stairways of faith and hope
that mother spoke of to her son
never to acquiesce her being
as a mere raisin in the sun,
I soared with wisdom and strength
from mrs. luella bates washington jones
who stood, who taught, who showed
that willow wild boy
and others to come
the way—
so we could one day say
thank you m'am
thank you langston.

Moving Day

Both women stopped and fiercely looked at each other. Lily looked at the ceiling fixture. Miss Ella, the older woman, turned her neck and studied the raveled piece of saddle tan carpet on her living room floor. After a few minutes, she put her eyes back on Lily.

"Seem that year you stayed on Richmond Place you had baby diapers decorating the floor like throw rugs. Days and days of leftover food in plates. And you had clothes everywhere. Hanging out closets. Hanging out dresser drawers. Hanging off arms of the couch. Hanging off doorknobs. Hanging . . ." The older women stopped and caught her breath.

Lily's mind went shameful. It left her face frozen with a muddled expression. The kind people get after too much music and too much liquor at a summer music concert.

"You taught me everything I know," Lily said, a humbled look in her eyes.

The older woman said nothing. She knew she had not taught her everything she herself knew. She knew that kind of knowledge could not be managed by a twenty-five-year-old. It had to be vesseled and placed in deep vats. Slowly, fermented and distilled in aged oak. By someone who had put in more time and years on this earth.

"I have to go and fill out some paperwork . . . Miss Ella . . . for my utilities," Lily managed meagerly to get the words out. It was the second of April when Lily first told her that she was going to move. She felt good that it had finally been said. She remembered when she had told her, Miss Ella had looked up with a frightened, ambivalent smile. She remembered how she leaned back in her cloth-like blue rocker. Her richly blackened and hardened feet, swollen from years of worry mixed with type II diabetes. The blood-thinning medicine she had taken for the past seventeen years did little to relieve the evidence of other people's burdens she had carried. Including her own children. Their children. And their children's children.

"And that joker laying around, lounging on that nice sofa sleeper you bought when you were working at the post office," Miss Ella replied, not finished with expressing her aging mind's walk down memory lane. "Why you wanna go and sling those kids around from school to school? They can't learn nothing that way."

"I ain't slinging my kids around no where." Lily shot back. "I told you this place has a real yard."

She emphasized "real" because she knew the yard was occasionally occupied with beer cans, abandoned cars, and other people's junk, barely enough room for Dennie and Della to go outside and play. Although Lily had been thrown out of her sore eye of an apartment in East Earlham Heights, she had no intentions of making 724 Apartment B Loveless Street her home. Now declaring to move in a house clear across Shoal Creek, taking her two children with her, she knew Miss Ella's heart felt as heavy as a bucket of lard.

"It's got a decent size backyard where the kids can play," Lily said.

"Lord, don't you neglect those children for some nogoodlowlife," Miss Ella said as she gritted her teeth, speaking just above a whisper.

"I ain't neglecting my kids for nobody." She knew the older woman cared for her dearly but hated her personal choices when it came to menfolk.

"I hope you take better care of Dennie. Maybe now you'll teach Della not to be so house-nasty with her bedroom." Lily's face looked with the same shamefulness she had shown after hearing the older woman's words about "hanging."

"I don't know where Della get her nasty ways from. She didn't learn it from me."

She looked at the floor not knowing where else to look. The older woman reached her hand on the duofold next to her rocker, grabbed the remote control, and clicked back to her morning game show. That kind of talk stirred her. Drops of sweat began to roll down her underarms. Then, she started tapping on her right thigh like she was trying to tell it something. She didn't want to think on this moving talk anymore. She tried to recollect her thoughts. But her mind starting racing so fast that her thoughts began peeling rubber. They finally came to a jostling halt and arrived at images of her crouched on a damp pantry floor near a sack of smelly russet potatoes. She was same age that Della was now.

Suddenly, still sitting in her chair, her mind wrapped and bound in an heirloom chest, she clutched her hands as if from enemy capture and became audience to scenes of past horror. She sat awhile longer in her rocker and thought to herself. She knew Lily's mind was bent on moving.

᙭   ᙭

Steve Whisnant

Confession of a Young Drunk

I averaged two to four drunken blackouts per week and drank five to six days out of any seven-day cycle. The population I put at risk from my consumption, you ask? This is my confession.

How no one got hurt, or worse, from my recklessness is a miracle. Friends riding shotgun claimed I followed traffic laws and drove safe. It's no excuse. I'm not proud of my immaturity and stupidity twenty years ago.

On one occasion I drove my truck into a ditch. My only memory of the rollover was grabbing the seat for dear life. I walked away without a scratch! The event occurred on a rural county road late at night, and I waited until I was sober before calling authorities.

Luck?

An old college buddy crashed his car into a teenager, killing the girl. His Glen Campbell-like drunken mug shot in the paper the next day will never be gentle on my mind.

The old gang from school commented how awful, and how could he do it? Ironic, don't you think, that we each had many opportunities to walk in his shoes had the stars aligned right. After all, it only takes one attempt to drive under the influence to hurt or kill someone. Studies show that a vast majority of the population has achieved this task—*even just one time*.

After graduate school, I worked for the Health Department's Bureau of Alcohol and Drug Abuse Prevention. Old friends who knew my past thought it funny (and paradoxical).

My drinking habits by now decreased from a daily drunk, to a weekend warrior, to an occasional beer sipper. Hank Williams Jr. had it right when he sang hangovers hurt more than they used to. Research shows most drinkers mature off alcohol and other drugs. The real alcoholics are the ones who continue. Rock bottom, baby!

The job was a daily catharsis. Yes, my alcoholic past was bad, but many directors of treatment centers and their counselors had it worse. It took a major event for them to achieve sobriety. Why do we have to be at our worst before seeing the light?

So, where is my confession leading? As a father of three daughters, I hope to protect the girls from drunk drivers and prevent my children from repeating my high-risk behavior.

And I don't mean prohibition of alcohol. That won't work. I mean to educate them on the proper way to drink without putting themselves and others in harms way. I'm a tough love advocate, as they will soon learn.

An old moral anecdote tells of a man on a beach, after a storm, throwing starfish that have washed ashore back into the ocean. A boy asks the elder what he's doing. "Putting the starfish back in the water so they won't die," the old man says.

"But there are thousands of them along the sand. You can't possibly make a difference."

The old man holds up the starfish in his hand. "I can for this one."

So what about you?

Do you know someone who might benefit from my confession? Tack the article on the bathroom mirror so he or she will see it in the morning while brushing teeth. Highlight a passage or two to draw his attention.

Demand that he not put society at risk from his drinking habits. And set an example yourself. Let's not be hypocrites. Let's use our own past to safeguard the future.

How would it feel to be in a courtroom with parents of a child you'd killed sitting behind you? Nothing you can say will be of consequence. You will have to live with your actions forever, while that deceased child will never experience the joy of life.

Until you can imagine yourself in this situation, nothing I say here will matter. So begin now. Sit in a quiet room and close your eyes. Pretend you just awoke from a blackout, and are lying on a bunk in the county detention.

The jailer looks at you from the other side of the bars. "Good goin', buddy. You killed a little girl and her mommy last night. Stupid drunk."

Keep your eyes shut. Now look around at the inmates you share the cell with. Do they think it's funny? What is their reaction?

Later, when you're released and arrive home, what do you do? Lie on the couch and watch TV? Is there a news story of what you've done with an interview of the little girl's dad? Maybe newsreels of you, drunk, being led into the county jail.

Keep going—don't let your imagination fail now. Use this newfound empathy to project yourself into a situation before it occurs.

The phone rings. "Mom?"

What do you say to her? What do you tell your friends at work on Monday?

Your wife or girlfriend walks in.

What do you tell her?

Later, in court, the police show enlarged photos from the crash scene. The prosecutor uses a laser pointer to exhibit where a chunk of engine smashed through the dashboard and cut open the mom's head. Brain matter is pushed out the gaping wound. The next image is that of the little girl. What does she look like?

Don't let your vivid imagination falter. What can two, several ton vehicles do when colliding? What can you do to prevent it?

War on Drugs

My essay here is not to change your mind that drug use is okay, but I do intend to persuade you that our approach in the War on Drugs will never win. We need something different!

That drug abuse causes harm in our society is indisputable. Look around: drunk drivers who kill innocent victims, family violence, fetal alcohol syndrome, AIDS from sharing needles, criminals intoxicated when breaking the law, tobacco deaths, injuries while under the influence, and on it goes. When you explore the costs associated with these examples, you realize this "war" is no minor event.

But does moderate, recreational *use* of drugs always cause harm? Can drug users enjoy their *medicine of choice* without hurting those around them?

Let's not split hairs here. Pharmaceutical substances, tobacco, and alcohol are all drugs, and we see a vast percentage of our population consume their legal drug of choice without causing destruction to society.

Of course, medical expenses increase from higher insurance rates after a lifelong use of tobacco and alcohol. Think lung cancer and cirrhosis of the liver. And the costs to purchase these items might be money better used for other family issues. This topic I'll save for another essay entitled: *Baby Needs New Pair of Shoes*. For now I want to focus on the immediate harm.

So could marijuana, cocaine, and heroin users enjoy their drug without causing damage? The answer is yes. In fact, I'll argue a single alcohol user on average will cause more destruction than a user of many prohibited drugs. Much of the crime committed by illegal users derives from their attempt to purchase the drug, such as in burglaries and robberies.

I propose our society adopt what is known as the Harm-Reduction theory. The premise is that we focus upon the harm instead of the actual use. I'm still an advocate of prevention and treatment, but our current War on Drugs has not worked. Incarceration is an expensive failure.

The goal in this "war" is to reduce the supply of illegal drugs, thereby causing an increase in the cost to purchase them. This will lead to decreasing numbers of users because they can't afford it. The Executive Office of the President, and Office of National Drug Control's own report, highlighted in their annual release, *Pulse Check*, shows that the supply and cost for illegal drugs has not decreased since the early 90s. It's been compared to assigning more and more men to put Humpty Dumpty back together again.

To throw illegal users in prison is an inhumane fiasco. Recidivism rates, which means the inmate is re-arrested within three years of his release, run at 60-80 percent, depending upon the crime. At an average annual cost of over $20,000 per prisoner, that's quite a failure.

Note that I'm not arguing from a "freedom" point of view. After all, in our "free" country, shouldn't I be able to smoke a joint or do a line of cocaine? But my support for this behavior stops when someone creates a harm.

Want to have a glass of wine—go for it. Want to hit a dubbie? Do it. But you better not put my family at risk because you had to drive down to 7-Eleven for a midnight munchies break!

There are books by scholars, and articles in popular journals such as the *New England Journal of Medicine*, that highlight many issues I discuss here. I'm not just making it up. Much of the damage from a drug like heroin comes from the way the drug is cut at the street-dealer level. The non-heroin products cause a lot of medical problems, as well as the means the users participate in to get the drug (e.g., robberies). But give them safe drugs and monitor their progress, most will not cause harm, and many will mature off, as they grow older. There are methadone programs now that try this approach.

When someone is arrested for a drug-related crime, often they are booked, jailed, then *back on the street in the same environment*. It may take months before his court date. Fortunately, in the past ten years there are now drug courts where offenders are funneled.

The premise here is that the arrestee is immediately sent before a judge with training in substance abuse, and will be interviewed and monitored by a court social worker. The user will be drug tested and if he breaks the rules or causes harm, he will then be sent to jail. Recidivism rates for these programs are often below twenty percent. Annual costs are much lower than prison. And, users are allowed to work, are at home with family, and basically remain a productive citizen.

In the early twentieth century, the Temperance Movement began the ban of alcohol in the United States. This led to the passage of the 18th Amendment that made alcohol sales illegal. What happened?

Crime increased and drinkers went underground. The amendment became so unpopular that it was repealed in 1933 by the 21st Amendment. If you understand how difficult it is to add an amendment to our Constitution, you will appreciate the significance of what happened.

The war has now moved from alcohol to other drugs. Many argue that our current battle against illegal substances began in the 60s with Nixon, or 80s under Reagan or Bush. Nope, it began way back around the passage of the Harrison Act in 1914. David Musto, a professor at Yale School of Medicine, wrote the best-known book on the subject entitled *The American Disease: Origins of Narcotic Control*.

He clearly shows our long-term policy to make certain drugs illegal has made things worse. Of course, I agree some hallucinogens should be banned. But for many drugs, the actual use is not what's harming our society. So light up, or sniff you a line. But don't screw up. That's where my support for you ends.

Zoom a Zoom and a Boom Boom

Walking past parked vehicles, Kyle and his three girls headed toward the YWCA on 12th and Cleveland for afternoon exercise. The siblings would remain with a sitter as Daddy hit the weights.

Barbara and Noelle, the four-year-old twins, ran after their older sister. "Be careful," Kyle yelled. "You don't want to trip on the concrete and hurt your knees."

Trying to keep up with the kids, Kyle paced around a truck idling along the fire lane near the front entrance. A mature gentleman carried stereo equipment through glass doors; Kyle held them open as his daughters and the man passed.

"Careful!" Kyle cautioned. "Let him in first."

In the lobby a group of senior women conversed near a water fountain. They wore formal gowns and dresses designed in a variety of fashions, and immediately caught the sisters' attention. Several distinguished gentlemen dressed in black slacks and dark shirts walked up the hall. Kyle was reminded of the *Dancing With the Stars* show.

As he scanned his membership ID card in at the front desk, he noticed a sign taped to the counter. "Ballroom Dancing from 5:00 to 7:00."

When he turned, he saw his daughters transfixed at the entrance to the main hall where couples could be seen twirling one another as they all danced around in what looked to be an organized circle.

"Let's go . . . you can play in the nursery."

With the sisters safe with a babysitter, Kyle entered the gym and warmed up on the stationary bike. Through a glass wall he could watch additional couples arrive in the main lobby. A few younger female participants caught his attention with their skimpy costumes, curved hips, and tight muscular legs with feet that slipped into high-heel shoes.

One duo strolled down the hallway dressed in western wear, she in a dress that ended above her knees and boots that covered most of her shins. He sported black jeans and rhinestone shirt with a black hat atop his head.

A wall clock read 5:00. Kyle noticed all the dancers disappear into the large auditorium. With the radio playing a rock station, he couldn't hear their dance music from down the hall.

At 6:00 he finished his workout and retrieved the girls. As they passed double doors to the auditorium, they saw forty or fifty dancers in synchronistic movements sweep back and forth upon hardwood floors.

The sisters ran to the open doors and stared in. A mature woman who looked over eighty moved to the side. She wore a long black dress with extensions from her sleeve that attached to her skirt and seemed to hold up the lace.

"Oh, you precious girls. Would you like to watch?"

They all nodded, so she moved to allow them in. Kyle followed and they stood just inside, along a wall. He felt awkward surrounded by such exquisite fashion while he wore maroon cotton sweats with perspiration stains along his collar.

Female dancers beside him discussed fabric with terms like Mysticwaves, Purple Reptile, Fuschia Splash, Blue Leopard, and Silver Swirls.

Dancers on the floor began to circle and Kyle noticed a man who looked to be in his late seventies beside a much younger woman. He wore tight black slacks that left little to the imagination. The pullover top hugged his chest and his baggy arms could be seen through slinky sheer sleeves.

His partner wore a two-piece silver and bronze outfit with tassels that defied gravity when she twirled. Her model-like face and hourglass figure made it difficult for Kyle to watch without feeling certain urges. A pierced bellybutton with a diamond-encrusted butterfly transfixed Kyle as he followed its every movement.

A lull broke the rhythm when CD music of some classical song ended. Dancers looked tired and many took a break. A gaggle of senior ladies who had flirted with the young sisters held out their hands.

"Let us show you how to step."

A few patrons sipping drinks watched. Kyle noticed how they smiled at the cute display of his daughters trying to perform. The guy at the stereo played some remix tune of a 50s song.

When the sound faded and the grownups said they needed to rest, the sisters stayed on the dance floor and held hands in a circle.

At first they skipped around emitting childish giggles, almost falling as the oldest pulled too fast at times. The seven-year-old then let go of hands and began to bump her rump against her twin siblings.

"Aren't they cute," a lady said to Kyle. "I have four grand children and I love them all so much."

What happened next surprised Kyle. His oldest daughter began to shake her hand in the air and yelled, "You gotta shake it like a Polaroid picture . . . " The twins imitated her.

They then shook their behinds back and forth and sang, "All I want is a zoom zoom and a boom boom . . . "

Kyle's eyes widened when he realized they had combined two rap songs that contained risqué lyrics. Dancers of all ages smiled and pointed, thinking it cute.

The female dancer with the incredible figure walked by, putting on a thin coat. "What kind of music are you letting them listen to? I hope no one here knows the symbolism with shaking like a Polaroid picture."

Kyle's face turned crimson. "I have no idea . . . "

She smiled. "And *Rump Shaker*? If these grandparents heard the entire song they'd be shocked. Kingston Trio never sang such stuff."

Tongue-tied, Kyle stared as his little girls continued to bump rears. "All I want is a zoom zoom and a boom boom . . . "

What was he going to do with the young rappers?

ॐ   ॐ

Shirley Smith Wilbert

Wisdom In Petunias

As bitter winter recedes,
barren terracotta vessels
await affiance with jaunty blooms,
Loam sifts through black and white fingers
like moments in time,
Planting season becomes
sharing secrets,
telling stories,
anticipating forever.

Showery springs
glowing summers lovingly minister,
Honeyed petunias flourish
with wild abandon,
All the while
lessons on life, friendship, pathos sustain

                                                               ‽   ℭ

C. A. Young

The Irony is That We Are All Hungry

I wonder as I stare into the soft
grey-blue of her eyes (cornea gone flat
and dull, obscuring the faint brown iris)
who she was and how she lived. How she died—

Well, that's obvious, isn't it? Any
layman can point to the region of the
Bite. That's how most of us are dying now.
not cancer or guns or disease. Just this.

The irony is that we are all hungry.
Just last week I ate what might have been the
last box of saltines on Earth for all I
know. This week? We'll run out of fruit cocktail.

Her eyes didn't change when I shot her. They
didn't dim. Didn't flinch. Didn't waver.

Pipe

'I need to take a
leak,' I remember he said to me.
A plumber. I was small.

'Can I watch?' I asked.
I didn't understand, I was from a
house full-up with women.

Years later, I remember silver
spots, burned into lino where the solder
fell, beads still brilliant coins.

That plumber's leak has plagued
me ever since, made me see the
plumbing as just that exactly.

I am suspicious and curious
upon encountering unfamiliar spigots on the sides
of office buildings . . . in public.

I think of copper pipes beneath
seersucker suits, marked by the downward
arrow of a bright silk tie.

PVC joints jostle in cotton briefs.
I chuckle in home repair stores,
my private joke made public.

I watch as other men in shops
brazenly handle elbow joints, fitter's cement,
tools of the trade, and I panic.

I can feel their fists,
the way they'd drag me into the
parking lot, and crush me.

They'd spill my blood with their
copper, lead, and plastic, wrenches and cutters,
over that other man's leak.

එ   ඎ

Jan L. Coffman

Mouse Bait

ଏ   ଓ

Appendices

Appendix A: Contributors

Evelyn Aholt

Evelyn Aholt was born the tenth of twelve children and lives in Glasgow, Missouri. She married her high school sweetheart and from their union came two daughters and two sons. Most of her time is devoted to her married children and their offspring. In addition to writing poetry and children's stories she enjoys quilting and crafting with her grandchildren. She has poetry published in various publications. Evelyn is a member of Columbia Chapter of Missouri Writers' Guild.

Larry W. Allen

Larry Allen is a Missouri probation/parole officer. He has had works published in *Mid-America Poetry Review*, *The Griffin*, *Fine Arts Discovery Magazine*, *NOW*, and previous issues of *Well Versed*. A poem is also forthcoming in *Main Street Rag* in 2010. Larry's book *"Do Come In" And Other Lizzie Borden Poems* was recently published by Pear Tree Press.

Edgar Bailey

Edgar Bailey, born a North Carolinian, is a Missourian by choice. Raised in various states in the continental United States and in one territory, he was privileged to attend eight schools in his first twelve years of education. His undergraduate degree is in humanities; graduate degree, public administration. He lives in Jefferson City with his lovely wife and his daughter's very demanding guinea pig.

Al Beck

His interests in life evolve from CURIOSITY, leading him onto fortuitous highways. A Korean War veteran, he was not prepared to ever again leave the USA, but graduate work at the University of Paris (Sorbonne) in France became a reality for travel abroad. His role as an art teacher began in 1956—moving from elementary to high school in Ohio to Dean at the Kansas City Art Institute and finished at Culver-Stockton College, retiring in the late 1990s. He was a Professor Emeritus volunteer educator after that. After retirement, he began to write poetry, song lyrics, essays, made drawings, unique clay vessels, tended a garden filled with heirloom vegetables, and continued performing with banjo as a Professional American Folksinger. His website identifies where he lives: www.rockyhollow.net.

J. M. Brandt

J.M. Brandt is tired of people online mistaking her for a man. She's been married for almost five years to the budding sociologist, Cowboy Joe. She works full-time at a local computer company and part-time in a hospital. Currently, she's learning Spanish against her will, but being able to read some of Pablo Neruda's poems makes up for it. She has a weakness for poems that have geology, dinosaurs, or B-movies in them.

Carol Gorski Buckels

Carol Gorski Buckels is a writer who dabbles in other art forms including photography and music (violin, fiddle, piano, harp and cello). She lives in Rocheport, Missouri, with her husband of twenty-three years. They share their home with three cheerful dogs and three fine cats. Carol's writing has appeared in *Well Versed, Show Me Missouri Women: Selected Biographies, Mid-Missouri Mature Living Magazine, Small Farm Today Magazine* and the *Columbia Business Times*.

Carol Buening

Inspiration presents her with a gift, sends her on a journey pursued. It becomes a poem, speech, creative fiction or non-fiction story, or a letter.

Thirty-five of her poems were published in *Well Versed*.

Performances include Newman Players, storytelling, literary readings, Toastmasters Club speeches and speech contests.

Past President of Columbia Chapter of Missouri Writers' Guild and long term member, past president of Columbia Toastmasters Club and Mid-Mo Advanced Toastmasters Club, a Distinguished Toastmaster and a founding member of Mid-Missouri Organization of Storytelling.

Barri L. Bumgarner

Barri L. Bumgarner has released numerous articles, short stories, and three novels. Her newest story, "Preconceptions," appears in the anthology *My First Year in the Classroom*. Her young adult novel, *Dregs*, tackles tough issues that lead to school violence, and was runner-up for the Walter Williams Major Work Award in 2008. Her first two books are award-nominated thrillers: *Slipping* and *8 Days*. Barri teaches at University of Missouri, while completing her PhD. www.barriLbumgarner.com.

Jimmy Capps

Jimmy Capps is old, fat, and ugly, when awake. When dreaming, he is young, slim, and handsome. He studied art and history at the College of the Ozarks, then traveled the world with the U.S. Navy, circling the earth five times. He returned to Missouri and lives near Versailles. He spent eight years in the State Penitentiary as an instructor. He is retired and a burden to his loving wife Kathryn. He has written hundreds of short stories, adding to them on a regular basis.

James H. Coffman

Mr. Coffman's poetry *Gravel Dust and Dreams*, was published in 2009, another, *Outside the Crowd*, will be released in 2010. He lives in Columbia, Missouri, with wife Janice.

Jan L. Coffman

Watercolors and pencil sketches were Jan's creative tools until she discovered digital photography. She creates her art photography by combining art skills with technology training. In addition to painting and sketching with the computer, she enjoys the untouched photograph. Jan taught learning disabled students and technology skills as an elementary school teacher. She is married to author and poet, James H. Coffman.

Cathrine Daily

Catherine Daily is working on two novels of a fantasy series with ideas for many more. Mostly she writes for fun and to stay sane. She lives in Columbia, Missouri, with her husband and five cats.

Elizabeth Davis

Elizabeth Davis writes "Historically Yours," a weekly column about the War Between the States, for the *Boonville Daily News*. She is also a regular contributor for the weekly column "Gift of Story." Her short story "When I Grow Up" was published in the CCMWG's annual anthology *Well Versed 2009*. Elizabeth has recently branched out into public speaking. She enjoys reading, listening to audio books, crocheting, music and, of course, writing.

Linda Fisher

Linda Fisher has been published in *Echoes of the Ozarks*, *Well Versed*, *A Cup of Comfort*, *Chicken Soup*, and created and edited *Alzheimer's Anthology of Unconditional Love: The 110,000 Missourians with Alzheimer's*. Her 2008 blog entries were published in *Early Onset Blog: Essays from an Online Journal*. Linda was the 2009 President of CCMWG. Her health blog is found at http://earlyonset.blogspot.com.

Grace Fogle

Grace Fogle is a high school freshman. In addition to writing and schoolwork, she spends her time on worthy causes such as saving endangered magical species.

Ida Bettis Fogle

Ida Bettis Fogle lives in Columbia, Missouri, with one husband, an assortment of pets and two food critics. Her writing has appeared in a number of places, including *Thema* and *The First Line*.

Lori Galaske

Lori fell in love with books at an early age, and began writing for the sheer joy of it at the age of twelve. After a brief hiatus from writing of thirty-five years, she attended The Institute for Children's Literature and graduated in 2008. Lori lives in Columbia with her high school sweetheart, Marc (who also happens to be her husband) and her empty-nest-therapy dog, Marje.

Svetlana Grobman

Svetlana Grobman is a Russian immigrant, an American librarian, and a freelance writer. In the nineteen years she has lived in the U.S., she has had many different experiences and has gone through a variety of changes.

Sharon Kinney Hanson

Sharon's first poem was published when she was a junior high school student. In college and thereafter, her poetry appeared in literary journals, including *River Styx*, *Helicon Nine*, *Sou'Wester*. Sharon has edited two anthologies, *Missouri*

Women Writers and *Memories and Memoirs,* and authored several titles, the latest being a biography, *The Life of Helen Stephens: The Fulton Flash* (Southern Illinois University Press, 2004).

Debra A. Hardin

Debra A. Hardin resides in Boone County, Missouri, having wound her way there through the back roads of America. Dealing with profound hearing loss, much of her current writing addresses the daily joys and sorrows of living and surviving in this hearing world.

C. B. O'Brien

C. B. O'Brien was born in San Francisco. A child of the 60s, he grew up in the Bay Area and was influenced by the two great events of that time—the war in Vietnam and the libertarian movement back home. Much of his poetry is a reflection of those influences. Although he has a few publications, poetry is mainly an activity of personal exploration.

Debbie Parker

Debbie Parker lives in Columbia, Missouri, with her husband and four-legged children. She works at the University of Missouri-Columbia and teaches in the Intensive English Program. Debbie is treasurer of the Columbia Chapter of Missouri Writers' Guild and has been published in the *St. Joseph Gazette, Columbia Magazine, Notable Missouri Women, Bliss-Parsons Journal of Metaphysics, Well Versed* and *Healing Talk.*

Teresa Shields Parker

lives in Columbia with her husband, Roy; son, Andrew; daughter, Jenny; two foster daughters and a mean cat named Darling. She holds a bachelor's degree in journalism/religion and a master's degree in theology. She has served as editor and publisher of several local publications and has written numerous nonfiction articles. A journalist for more than 30 years, she is now trying her hand at fiction.

Von Pittman

Von Pittman specializes in locating the most obscure publications possible for his short stories and reviews. He hopes that his fiction is more believable than many of the reports and strategic plans to which he has contributed in his work as a career university bureaucrat. He reviews mysteries and thrillers for the Web Site *The GenReview*.

Cate Richard

Cate Richard has over twenty years' experience working in the publishing industry as both writer and editor. She has written and published six books, one of which, *Miss Cornett's Courtship*, has been compared to a novella version of the best-selling *Cold Mountain*. Before buying Romancing the Past Bed & Breakfast and relocating to Fulton, Missouri, she lived in Los Angeles, California, where she wrote and marketed several of her award-winning screenplays.

Eva Ridenour

Eva Ridenour started her writing career by writing magazine articles. She has written and published eight novels under the pen name of Elizabeth Butler. *Libby* is the 2004 Walter Williams Award winner of the Missouri Writers' Guild. Her poetry has appeared in *Cappers, The Mid-America Poetry Review* and *Well Versed*. She is past-secretary and president of CCMWG and past-treasurer of the Missouri Writers' Guild. A retired secretary from Illinois, she lives in Armstrong, Missouri. Her web site is www.elizabethbutlers.com.

William Edward Samuels

William Edward Samuels a free lance writer and native of Columbia whose works have been published in *The St. Louis*

Post-Dispatch, Writers On The River, Educational Freedom, The Tennessee Star, local newspapers and elsewhere. He is also an attorney and former visiting law professor in Russia with the Yale affiliated Civic Education Project. His novel, *Project Platinum* has been copywrited and self published.

Veronica Strega

Veronica Strega has won awards from the Academy of American Poets and PEN. She writes erotic fiction and poetry for *Clean Sheets*. She regularly contributed to the *Boston Phoenix* as a rock critic. She hosts "Anything Goes" on radio station kopn.org, frequently airing interviews with artists from The Grateful Dead family among others. She is writing a biography. Contact her at www.soulfoodflower.com.

Swiftwalker

Swiftwalker is the Lenape name of a retired professor of sociology who has written extensively on sickness, behavior and health care systems. His poetry has appeared in *Blue Unicorn, Off the Coast, Inside Sweden, Well Versed, Stanza,* and other venues. He lives in Columbia, Missouri, and East Boothbay, Maine, at the edge of the sea. He has been married 47 years to the same woman, who bore two children who, in turn, provided five beautiful grandchildren. Life is good.

Cathy Thogmorton

Cathy Thogmorton currently works as editor of *The Talon* magazine, a publication of Central Methodist University in Fayette, Missouri. She previously taught high school English in Lee's Summit, Missouri, for 25 years, and then wrote freelance for several years. She has written for a variety of publications, including *Missouri Life* magazine. She is currently writing her first novel.

Martin Turner

Martin Turner is a farm boy who went away to college. At the age of 48 he went back to the farm where he grew up and spent the next 15 years raising cattle. Since retiring in 2008 he has started writing poetry again.

Lar Glendal Wallace

Lar Glendal Wallace is a poet, writer and workshop presenter. She has taught English as a public school educator in the Midwest for twenty years. Most of her published work has been written for professional journals and local poetry venues. A lover of all things creative, she has recently relocated to the Pacific Northwest where she teaches at a community college and spends time enjoying mountain views as she continues to nurture her creative self.

Steve Whisnant

Steve Whisnant is a happily married father of three daughters, and has also been blessed with over 100 writing contest wins. He is past president of Fiction Writers of Central Arkansas, and member of the Ozarks Writers League, Northeast Texas Writers' Organization, Kansas Authors Club, and Columbia Chapter of the Missouri Writers' Guild. He has published two anthologies of his award-winning stories, a novel, and a children's book. His website is: www.stevewhisnant.com.

Shirley Smith Wilbert

Shirley Smith Wilbert retired, moved to Columbia, Missouri, and began writing poetry as an experiment. She has been published in *Well Versed, Peninsula Pulse, New Mirage Quarterly, Mid-America Poetry Review, Wisconsin Review,* and a chapbook, *Moon's Harp.* She is a member and former President and Secretary of CCMWG.

She received the Editor's Choice Award from the International Library of Poetry in 2005, and Writer's Digest Writing Competitions honors in 2005 and 2007.

C. A. Young

C. A. Young grew up in a small town where he developed a love of aesthetic decay and a desperate need to live somewhere bigger. He lives and writes in Columbia, Missouri, where he shares a house with his family and a pack of dogs. His work has most recently appeared in *Crossed Genres* magazine, and in Costcom Entertainment's zombie poetry anthology *Vicious Verses and Reanimated Rhymes*.

Appendix B: Columbia Chapter of the Missouri Writers Guild

Board of Directors, Columbia Chapter of the Missouri   Writers' Guild

Larry Allen, president
Judy Stock, vice president
Shawnna Matteson, secretary
Cathrine Daily, treasurer
Carol Buckels, administrator assistant
Lori Galaske, membership chair
Evelyn Aholt, member-at-large

Critique Leaders

James Coffman, poetry
Cathrine Daily, prose

The Write Direction Conference Committee

All officers
Eva Ridenour, publicity

Well Versed Committee

Judy Stock, chair
Linda Fisher
Eva Ridenour

༄   ༄

Appendix C: Our *Well Versed* Sponsors

The Columbia Daily Tribune
Sponsor

Mozark Press
www.mozarkpress.com
publisher@mozarkpress.com

Rock Springs Review
a small literary magazine
rsrev@sbcglobal.net

University of Missouri High School

Austin/Barkley Publishers
Champ Pike

୫୦   ୦୨

Appendix D: Submission Guidelines
for *Well Versed*

2011 *Well Versed* Submissions and Contest

Great prizes!

The Columbia Chapter of the Missouri Writers' Guild invites area writers to submit their original poetry, fiction and/or nonfiction manuscripts to be considered for publication in *Well Versed - 2011*. Submissions are automatically entered into the *Well Versed* Contest.

Our guest judges select manuscripts for publication and prizes. Prizes awarded to the Editor's Picks: $50 first place, $30 second place, $20 third place, and certificates for honorable mentions. The contest is <u>free</u> for CCMWG members.

For complete guidelines visit http://columbiawrites.coin.org and click on Submissions. The closing date for manuscripts to be considered for the 2011 edition is October 31, 2010.

৪০   ৫৪

Appendix E: The Write Direction Conference

Save the Date!
October 23, 2010

The 2010 Write Direction Conference
Columbia, MO

For more information or to register for the conference visit

http://columbiawrites.coin.org

ౙ ಚ

Appendix F: How to Become a Member of CCMWG

Membership in the Columbia Chapter of the Missouri Writers' Guild is open to all writers or aspiring writers.

Our membership meetings are normally the first Sunday of the month, 2 – 4 P.M., Orr Street Studios, Columbia. Please visit http://columbiawrites.coin.org to see the schedule. The meetings alternate between speakers and critique groups for prose and poetry. CCMWG holds a members-only meeting in September, but visitors are welcome at all other meetings.

Membership dues are $15.00 annually, payable in January. You may join at a monthly meeting or mail your check with complete contact information to:

Membership Chair
PO Box 7628
Columbia, MO 65205-7628.

Members who join after October 1 will have dues prorated the following year.

CCMWG members receive a discount for the annual Write Direction Conference and pay no fee to submit manuscripts to the annual *Well Versed*.

The chapter's members include many talented writers. Invest in your writing future and join CCMWG.

ဢ ∽